girl almighty

Jen Handoko

To Mom and Dad

CONTENTS

"Everything was brighter and more colorful in those years, as if my childhood was ending in an explosion of unreal passion that made my life feel sacred and holy."

— Roman Payne

GIRL ALMIGHTY

My mind has always been full of shallow things. As a child I had to read things twice or more because my brain couldn't retain information. Math gave me anxiety. Science was interesting until letters and equations came into the picture. I was average at spelling, I guess, but once came close to being the spelling bee champion in the third grade until I misspelled the word *condemned*. I never made it as magna cum laude in high school, but a girl named Eliza did and her graduation speech was long, uninteresting and lacked creativity. The entire time I thought I could have done a better job, but nobody would ever believe that a C student like me had anything inspiring or thoughtful to say.

Stories. I was good at telling stories and regurgitating facts about pop culture. For instance, I knew that Courtney Love was born in California and became a stripper at sixteen years old. She was the lead singer in a band called Hole and I came across their second studio album *Live Through This* at thirteen years-old when my best friend let me borrow her mom's copy. I spent months listening to it on a portable CD player. The moment the disc spun, the initial strumming of the song "Violet" began and I was enticed immediately almost every time. Her music sounded so foul and unclean, her vocals were snarling and angry, her lyrics—although cryptic and nonsensical at times—were the true words of a woman scorned. If I had to psychoanalyze myself, I'd assume that her music resonated with me because of the immense amount of pressure and lack of self-worth I felt as a child, as a girl. I didn't want to be raised as a self-respecting young lady. I wanted to frighten people with the rot in my chest, rip it out, and put it on exhibit.

One aspect of Love's psyche that I admired was the unwavering feminism. I found it interesting even as a child how her drug addiction was often ridiculed whereas if she were a man, the same drugs would have made her personality more interesting and prophetic. During a time when women in the music industry were virginal and pure, she committed the cardinal sin of being at the opposite end of the spectrum. She was unpolished and unapologetic. She implored women of the nineties to start their own bands instead of being groupies. She dug her heels in a male dominated scene. She wore baby doll dresses and screamed about the dichotomies that raged inside of her. It prompted me to want the martyrdom of being a powerful woman.

As a child of first-generation immigrants, you have a big responsibility to be great. We feel the pressure to compensate for the sacrifices that our parents made for us. We must spend the rest of our lives trying to provide something that will prove to our parents that their giant leap of faith was all worth it. After all, this *is* America, and it's only because of my parent's bravery that their daughters are free to say whatever we want and do whatever we want. *Be* whoever we want. My sisters and I watched our parents work hard despite them knowing very little English. They didn't have grandeur dreams. They wanted a nice home and food on the table. But what will my parents do once they've learned that one of their daughters just wants to be Courtney Love?

My aunt had neon orange press-on nails that dug into the muscle of my cheeks as she asked me a very important question: *What do you want to be when you grow up?* It was strange enough as a child to have relatives and authority figures ask such a critical question. But it was even stranger—frightening—to look inwards for a definitive answer. I didn't have an answer. I'd always shrug at the question asked by curious adults looking to start conversation. It was a question persistently on my mind that I spent most of my childhood (and, well, adulthood) repressing, waiting to be sorted out later. Whenever the question was being asked, I spent hours living in terror, having my first existential crisis during my dad's 50th birthday party. *Doctor?* Mom would love it but, no. Not my thing. *Veterinarian?* Maybe. I did have an admiration for animals. I enjoyed how they made me feel. But I was there when a vet had to put my dad's German Shepard down and it was the one and only time I ever saw my dad cry. I decided right then that I couldn't bear to see the darker parts of veterinary. The medical field is much more practical. Lawyer. Business owner. Become a nurse. These are cut-and-paste things: you go to school, get a degree, make tons of money and make your parents proud. None of it had to do with hope or chance. *All you have to do is put in the hard work*, I'd hear my mom say. I knew this. But no matter how much I knew wanting to find a career in the creative field was an impractical, overly ambitious desire, it didn't take away from the fact that I was really running out of options for myself. Nothing interested me.

I was late to register for school for my freshman year of high school, so I couldn't take the classes I wanted, like French or Drama. The only two classes left that weren't full were gym class or creative writing. Sweating before noon and smelling like the musty rankness of the great outdoors sounded miserable, so gym class was nixed. I had no other option but to be put into a writing class held in a trailer behind the gymnasium. My teacher's name was Mr.Simons and he played 80's new wave music during class. We learned that he loved cats, owned several of them, and walked around cemeteries recreationally.

One thing about his teaching that I am grateful for is how he forced us to be vulnerable. He always made us read our writing out loud. Up until that point, I'd never done that. My writing had always been for my personal use only. I began journaling and writing in diaries when I was ten years old. My mom gave me ten dollars to spend at my school's book fair and I bought myself a journal. I'd write in it whenever someone or something upset me: after an argument with my mom, after my dad lashed out on me, whenever my sisters brought boys home when our parents weren't around, or the one time our bald neighbor yelled at me for letting our dog shit in his yard, etc. But writing in my journal was a way for me to self-soothe, a healthy way to compartmentalize and process my emotions. I'd write about moments of happiness, too. I remember riding my bike on a Saturday morning in the spring time and the fresh scent of laundry wafted throughout the entire neighborhood. Cherry blossom petals covered the cars after light rain. Documenting the beautiful things made it easier for me to remember the times I felt happy and alive.

By high school, I was reading my darkest thoughts out loud to an entire class and I enjoyed it. Mr.Simons would allow people to offer advice or feedback after our readings and the senior kids would always give their praise to me. Once, in a highly depressive state, I wrote about wanting to commit suicide by running the engine of my dad's car inside the garage. I left it open on Word document and my dad read it. "I don't know what's wrong with you or if you were being serious," he began. "But I wanted to let you know that you're really good at this." The one and only time my dad ever gave me praise was when I wrote about dying in the driver's seat of his Jeep while my lungs filled up with carbon monoxide, just like the poetic way Kirsten Dunst's character did in the *Virgin Suicides*.

But the most monumental moment for me was Ben. I had a crush on a blonde-haired boy named Ben who sat next to me in Mr.Simons' class. He'd pick me up at my house before school started and we ate breakfast and smoked cigarettes before first period. Then he left me for a new girl. So, on Valentine's Day, I wrote a very bitter piece of writing about Ben in our creative writing class. Mr.Simons called on me to read my poem to the class and I made my way to the front of the room, cleared my throat, and read the entire thing out loud with Ben sitting in the front row. I noticed how he sank in his seat and his cheeks turned red. I watched him recoil in embarrassment. This fueled me.

As a girl, our demons are harder to make docile. Boys are told to silently internalize theirs while ours are free to roam like vagabonds. As freeing as it sounds, girls are told to *express* their emotions, but we're never taught how to healthily administer them. While my dream boy sank in his seat from my words, something clicked: writing was a powerful tool, a way to gain narrative coherence of my own life. Instead of taking my own life with exhaust fumes in my dad's garage, I vowed to stay and spend the rest of my years studying my demons and calling them by their names. Writing helped me understand them and I wondered if writing about mine could help others understand theirs.

There are many avenues in life one may take, but I never asked to be born so for the longest time I had trouble understanding why I was forced to decide which one to take. My birth was a cosmic mess forced upon me by two people, unknowingly. Perhaps my unplanned existence or my purpose in life is far bigger than anything my parents ever imagined; being an unplanned pregnancy meant that something bigger than my parents *wanted* me here. I'd spend most of my life figuring out what that is. It wasn't until my high school creative writing class and meeting Ben that it became so clear to me. I didn't have to be Courtney Love. I already possessed the almighty powers of being a woman. This book is the product of harnessing and making use of my traumas and issues. These are stories about certain events that I hadn't yet processed until the making of this book. This is an overdue homage to certain individuals and events that helped my own character development, even if they didn't mean to.

I wrote about my past so that I may have the freedom to redirect my future. I hope, in some way, my stories can inspire you to tell yours, too.

THE NOODLE GIRL

If I think about it long enough, I can still smell the earthy sweet cowhide of my dad's leather jacket and how it soaked up the stench of curry and cigarettes—its pungency, particularly when riding with him in the car. On school nights when I should be in bed, he'd always ask me if I wanted to come with him to pick my mother up from the train station. On these night drives, he'd play all his favorite music which was also indicative of what kind of mood he was in: saxophone love songs if he was stressed, stadium rock if he was happy. It was always either Kenny G's *Greatest Hits* album or Queen's *A Night at the Opera*.

When we reached the train station, he'd park the car (a dingy 1992 Mazda MPV that squealed when making turns) where it'd be most visible and smoked Marlboro Reds until her train arrived. Through the layer of frost on the window, I would watch four or five trains empty out and scan the crowd until I recognized my mom. She worked part time at a mall food court, offering samples of teriyaki chicken on toothpicks. Dad worked two part-time jobs; one at a bagel shop where he'd have to wake up at 5:30 a.m. every morning. At night, he'd deliver pizza. Sometimes, I would pretend I was asleep in the backseat. Mom would always play along with it:

"Oh, is my pretty girl sleeping?"
I'd slightly open my eyes for a subtle peek but never answer.

"Well, that's a shame. I managed to get my hands on the last Cinnabon before the food court closed. It'd be such a waste to throw it away, wouldn't it?"

I'd try to contain my giggling until I'd surrender into a chortling hysteria, erecting from my pretend slumber. She'd act surprised as if she didn't know I was awake the entire time, my dad would laugh, and they'd get a kick out of it before moving on to more serious conversations amongst themselves. She handed me the cold cinnamon roll wrapped in white napkin and I'd eat the congealed sugar off the top. I'd listen to music while they had conversations about things I didn't understand, usually finances.

Before she would even get out of her work clothes and decompress, she'd make a late dinner for me, my dad, and my two older sisters, Indah and Winny. She'd usually cook from the recipes that were handwritten in her red moleskin notebook that she inherited from her mother before we migrated to the United States in 1994. When she was too tired to cook anything extravagant, dinner would usually consist of noodles and fried eggs. It was cheap, quick, and the leftovers could last us until the next day, so it was also an economical choice.

My sisters—who were just teenagers at the time—would eat just a few bites before retiring back to their rooms to watch music videos on MTV. This was around the time when people could solely tune in to that particular channel for music—before reality shows starring pregnant teens and aggressively masculine Italian Americans from New Jersey infiltrated the schedule. I could hear the beginning of the wistful strumming of Smashing Pumpkin's single *1979*. I remember watching the music video and seeing Billy Corgan's thumb-like head somberly singing in the back of a 1972 Dodge Charger and scenes of teenagers doing donuts in an empty parking lot, the innocence of being a teenager in the 90's.

My mom was always the last one to eat. I'd watch the way she ate her food – the Indonesian way. With her right hand, she'd form a ball out of rice and protein to eat and then she'd bite into a red pepper. Once the spiciness became too overpowering, she'd finish with a bite of a chilled cucumber to ease the heat. My dad would coat his food with *sambal* to make his food even spicier despite evident perspiration at the table.

The next morning, I woke up to the same smell of garlic and pepper. Following the sound of oil popping, I found my mom in the kitchen reheating the noodles from the night before in an oversized wok. She'd put it in Tupperware and pack it with plastic utensils in my Hello Kitty tin lunchbox. She firmly believed that the lunch they served in public schools was just processed junk with absolutely no nutritional value. She would often describe it as *makanan penjara* which literally translates to "jail food".

To get to my school, my mom and I had to take a bus and walk the last few miles on foot because my father needed the car to deliver food. I remember how frigid the February air was and how every second that the wind didn't sting my cheeks was a moment of sweet relief. I would jump into a puddle of half melted snow and get mud all over my boots. She would grab my arm and tell me to behave for the last mile.

My elementary school was warm and colorful, a place where my numb, cold hands could instantly raise to normal body temperature and I'd be greeted with smiling, happy faces. I didn't mind being there once the separation anxiety wore off. I was obedient and smart, always receiving adoration from teachers. They would often tell me that I looked like a China Doll because of my thick, straight-across bangs and my blue-black hair braided neatly in a red velvet bow with tiny pearls. My mom, no matter how tired she was, always made sure there was enough time in the morning for this kind of primping. She was dedicated to presenting me to the world as well-groomed and as hyper-feminine as possible.

School wasn't always ideal, however, especially on the first day of 3rd grade when nobody knew how to pronounce my name. My teacher, Ms. Malcolm, was middle-aged, plump, and wore thick bifocals. Some kid made up a rumor that her husband left her at the altar at her wedding, which is the reason why she was so stern and mean. Her breath had the remnants of black coffee and her perfume smelt like star anise and licorice. It still wafts into my memory from time to time. She hovered above us at the dead center of the classroom and called attendance with a wooden clipboard. She called most names with ease:

"Sarah?"

Here.

"Julian?"

Present.

"Ian?"

Right here.

And then, the alphabet ascended to the letter G and I knew it was coming. She'd squint her eyes at my name on the clipboard during a long pause. I watched as the confusion grew stronger on her face. She stuttered different variations of my name, enunciated the G sound with a soft G like *giraffe* instead of the hard G like in *ghost*. Without correcting her, I yelped, "Here!" as quickly as I could so that she'd move on to the next name. I could hear a few kids guffawing: "What? Genghis?" Or another kid would say, "Guinness? Like the book of world record?"

Christina. I wanted to be a Christina. Whenever I would express this, my mom and I were at odds. "Gendis is more beautiful," she'd say. "It means sugar." It was true: I was born with a sweet tooth. When my parents weren't looking, I'd climb on top of the 50-pound bag of jasmine rice that boosted me onto the kitchen countertops to access the cabinet with sweetened condensed milk. Once, while my mom was recovering from stomach surgery, I found a bottle of fuchsia pink pills and sucked the semi-sweet coating off each one. I had a rotten tooth at seven years old. Gendis *was* the perfect name for me. But how could she have known about my affinity for sweets? Was this a predisposition? It still remains an enigma to me. I loved the way my mom said my name; how it rolled off her tongue in her dialect, the right way, like it was always meant to sound.

My classmates were either rowdy or had emotional issues, so in no time at all the teachers appreciated that I was one less thing to worry about. I became the star child despite being the girl with the weird name. One time, a kid named Matthew (a scratchy voiced boy who always had stains on his Old Navy t-shirt) informed the class that something smelled weird. "I think it's Gendis!" he announced, with his shirt covering his nose. I didn't know if it was the yellow curry from the night before or the olive oil hair elixir from my mother's collection of potions. Everybody snickered. I remember being so furious at my mom because this wasn't the first time that I was ridiculed for casting foreign odors. One hot Georgia summer, my mother brought home a dozen overripe durian fruits, which, essentially, are thorny fruits the size of cantaloupes with a custardy inside that smells like onions and feet. If you consume it, you'll burp onion feet for two days. The smell of the Indonesian fruit is so pungent, that it is banned in public transport in some Asian countries. Evidently, the stench also seeps easily into clothing. When I came home from school that day, I cried in my bedroom with the door locked.

But, the worst part of school was when it was time for lunch. By noon, my stomach sounded like it was eating itself, making noises like a possessed banshee. Sometimes, it wasn't so bad because it was when we would all trade food and show off our snacks. One day, my mom packed her infamous noodles. The moment I opened the lid to my container, smoky ribbons of steam were released in the air and everyone immediately looked in my direction and started dissecting my food with their eyes. One boy named Jesse—whose mother only ever packed him Reese's Puffs cereal in a Ziploc bag and a Yoohoo for lunch— scooted his chair far away, squeaking the metal of the chair legs across vinyl composition tile.

"What *is* that?" he asked, disgusted, face scrunched.

"I'm sorry," my shoulders dropped.

"I can move if you want."

When this encouraged more kids to express odor-based slurs, I placed everything back in the box and moved to the opposite end of the cafeteria table where nobody sat. I dissociated myself from everyone else with "normal" and "non-smelly" food and wished I, too, could eat cafeteria pizza with the cheese that tasted like plastic. I went on the rest of the day with an empty stomach.

When I came home that day, I opened the refrigerator and pushed the lemongrass and scallions out of the way for a Yakult drink, a yogurt probiotic drink that my mom would keep well-stocked. In the kitchen, my mom heard my stomach growling and she asked if I wanted her to fry some *pastel ayam*, a Portuguese-inspired dish from

Indonesia that comprised of pie crust stuffed with vermicelli, chicken, and vegetables. I shook my head.

"No? But that's your favorite." she wondered.

A moment goes by.

"Well, did you finish your lunch?"

I nodded my head, lying to her only because I knew how upset she'd be if she knew I didn't eat. She investigated inside my lunchbox and saw a full container of the lunch she prepared for me.

"Gendis, you wasteful child! You're going to finish this for dinner."

"I don't want to eat this nasty food!" I retorted.

She grimaced.

"Why can't you make me ham sandwiches like my friends?" I groaned.

"Because I am not like their mothers. I'm yours. Go join another family if I'm so bad!"

That was a popular thing my mother seemed to enjoy using as a threat. It was strange because, on one hand, the fantasy of living next door at the O'Neil's house seemed pretty sweet. They got to watch *Nick at Night* until 10:30 p.m. on a school night and could play outside long after the streetlights come on. On the other hand, it wasn't realistic. As unfair and weird as my household was, I was bound to my family by homesickness.

Things got a little better once another foreign student—a Vietnamese boy named Binh—was introduced to our class one morning. He spoke absolutely no English whatsoever and although this was understood, my teacher still spoke in a fast, Southern drawl which he could never

15

understand. She then began to talk slowly, more condescending, and with more hand movements. This was still just as confusing and stressful to Binh. His chubby cheeks were now flushed with a cherry hue when everyone in the class giggled every time he couldn't reply to her. We had an assignment about our favorite things to do in the summer. Ms. Malcolm asked him, "Do you like to swim?"

"Swim." he repeated.

"Yes, swim. Do. You. Know. How. To. Swim?" she asked, mimicking a butterfly stroke.

"Swim." he repeated again.

Ms. Malcolm flung her arms in the air and looked at me.

"Gendis, do you know how to speak his language?" she asked.

"No, ma'am, I'm Indonesian."

"What do they speak in Indonesia?"

"Indonesian."

I felt really bad for Binh sometimes, especially when it was time to play dodgeball in the gymnasium, and he didn't understand why pelting rubber balls at unfathomable speeds was a recreational activity. Even if he wanted to play, none of the boys liked him enough to choose him on their team. As a result, he was always the last one to be picked. Because of this, Coach Spaulding would usually put him in the girl's team to even out the number. He usually sat down and pulled the green from the Astroturf.

Things got better for Binh and even better for me when another foreign exchange student came into our classroom. Her name was Chen and she was from China.

She spoke moderately good English and a lot of classmates liked her because she had beautiful cursive handwriting and brought fortune cookies on Valentine's Day. At lunch, people were fascinated by her chopsticks. She offered a kid named Frederick one of her pork dumplings. Fred made a face, stopped chewing, and spat it onto his plate. Everyone laughed. I saw the fire growing in her eyes.

Every October, the school hosted International Night which was an after-school event that was dedicated to celebrating all countries and cultures. Mom made my favorite noodles and *nasi goreng*, an Indonesian-style fried rice dish. Dad let me borrow a colorful tapestry of intricate batik patterns to put on our station and brought his Wayang Dolls; scary, lanky, androgynous wooden puppets from the island of Java. They had white faces, red lips, and thick black mustaches not unlike a cross-dressing Lucifer. A lot of parents and teachers came up to my mother and complimented her cooking. They praised her, which always brought a glow to her face. She loved the appreciation because it made her feel a sense of belonging in a community that she was an alien to. Seeing her happy made me happy. It was as if the weirdness that I was born into was finally something to be proud of and not ashamed about. I noticed that Jesse finished his entire plate of spicy noodles. I ran up to him and said, "You said it looked gross and smelly." He gulped the last bit of food down his throat. "I've always wanted to try it, but I was too shy to ask."

My sisters didn't seem to have any issues at their high school, none whatsoever. Contrary to my experience, it was ironically the same culture that made them stand out from the rest of the girls at their school. My sisters were popular—Winny being the most social and funny, and Indah always had boyfriends that ended up being obsessed with her, so much that we had to change our home number because of incessant calls from a stalker, and so much that I threatened one of her boyfriends with a box cutter when he brought her home past curfew. Boys would always buy her rose bouquets and Ferrero Rocher chocolate and she'd be apathetic towards such acts of kindness. Sometimes, on rare occasions, my parents would allow me to visit Winny at school. I would sit in her biology class and all her friends would braid my hair and say "Aww! Your little sister looks exactly like you!"
I think she enjoyed the attention and so did I. It was a symbiotic relationship. Our resemblance was uncanny; my sisters and I all had our father's full lips and our mother's cheekbones. Indah, the oldest, had D-cup breasts at 15. Winny was bottom heavy and had long brown hair that glistened like molasses in the sun. Although the admiration over them was abundant, it was mainly fetishized as if they were a special token or exotic fruit at the highest branch of a tree, soaking up all the sunshine.

What our family had experienced that nobody knew much about were the sacrifices we had to face. Because we were illegal immigrants, we couldn't travel back to Indonesia often. I came into the living room one night and saw my mother hiding her face in one hand and holding the phone receiver in the other. Her father was going to pass away, but she was unable to fly back, fearful that she wouldn't be able to get back into the U.S if she did. She could only hear the details of her father's passing through the phone. She said her last exchange of words with him through a 6-minute long distance phone call.

To make ends meet, she began to cater food (without a license) out of our own kitchen and came across an opportunity to cater food for the Indonesian athletes for the 1996 Summer Olympics in Atlanta. They paid her enough to put a down payment on a house in a quaint neighborhood. This was obviously a monumental moment for my parents. They saved just enough money to move us out of our small apartment and into a nicer neighborhood. It was a red brick 3-bedroom home with a white picket fence and a big, creepy basement. The front lawn was lush, an ideal place for the usage of plastic flamingos for decoration like normal Americans. But my mom was persistent about using traditional Indonesian parasols instead, adorned with gold and red tassels. I thought it was strange and ridiculous, especially when our neighbors would ask what they were, politely, with a hint of condescension. Whenever I came to my mom with these concerns, she laughed and said, "No, these are beautiful!" and so she had it her way.

When my dad decorated the living room with dragon heads carved from Balinese teakwood, I drew the line. The demonic looking decorations with red eyes and long curly tongues startled my friends. I just didn't understand why we couldn't decorate the damn place with normal things, like, you know, taxidermy. A stuffed deer head looming above the fireplace would have somehow made the room more rustic and cozy, unlike these gargoyles.

"Don't disrespect Barong like that," he began to warn me. "He will hear you."

"Who?" I asked.

"These little guys represent good and evil. They help protect our home."

"Whatever."

I would take them all down and hide them in cabinets.

Periodically, I would fight him over custody of the gargoyles. I desperately tried to convince my parents to redecorate our home like how most Southerners do: red and white gingham tablecloths, ceramic roosters, freshly cut gardenias as centerpieces. Yet, despite my wishes, the Javanese handicraft remained intact.

When I reached the 6th grade, nobody could pronounce my name correctly; nevertheless, still using the soft G sound. I was knighted with the name *Jen* out of convenience by classmates and teachers. At the time, I wasn't bothered by it and certainly was not concerned with my lack of integrity of allowing people to erase my culture. To younger me, it was the first time I could be addressed by a name that I didn't have to constantly correct. I became somewhere between tolerant and apathetic. *Jen. Jenny From Da Block. Jen-Jen. Jennifer.* It became a part of my identity for the rest of my youth and, unknowingly, my adulthood. It was the metamorphosis from the weird foreign girl to a normal, average American girl next door. The popular girls thought I was pretty after I begged my mom to let me get chunky blonde highlights. I only wore distressed denim skirts and collared shirts from Abercrombie & Fitch. I made the cheerleading squad that year. I kissed a boy that wasn't mine. I threw a Halloween party that the older kids even came to.

Only until the better part of my adulthood was there a notable shift in the American perspective on Asian culture. When my mother saw the 2010 film *Eat, Pray, Love*, I remember how she was so elated to see her country being depicted in Hollywood as an ethereal, spiritual place. What I didn't know was that, in the future, it's now a place where Instagram influencers and "brand ambassadors" go to retrieve aesthetic creative content. Bali, Indonesia will suddenly be on everyone's bucket list—a honeymoon destination for couples who want to seem worldly or spiritually awakened. This phenomenon is bizarre to me: all it took was for America's sweetheart Julia Roberts to make South Asia instantly trendy. My country, a place where nobody could point out on a globe, was now a place for newly divorcees to embark on a quest to "find themselves". It's now daring to step out of comfort zones. But this circumstance was not necessarily true 15 years ago when my family was facing xenophobic neighbors and coworkers. None the less, this peculiar feeling I have with the irony of it all often coincides with the gratitude I have that there's now more tolerance and interest about my cultures. In the future, my American friends and I will stumble out of bars and someone is always bound to say, "You know what I could really go for right now? A hot bowl of pho." When this happens, everyone in the group will hold their stomachs and exclaim, "Oh fuck, me too" and so here we are, slurping noodles at 3 a.m. I remember my mom making pho for us during the cold winter months and my neighbor complained about the smell. Now, noshing away at gentrified Vietnamese food is a bonding experience with my American friends.

* * *

I've never been a fan of sports but sometimes soccer reminds me of the Saturday mornings when my dad would drift in and out of sleep on his dual recliner in the living room with FIFA World Cup blaring loudly. In between his snoring (that sounded like someone sawing wood) and the enthusiastic *GOOOOAAL!!* from the Latin sports commentator, I'd stick my head out of my bedroom door and yell, "I'm trying to read, you know!" and slam the door as hard as I could. Recently, I agreed to attend an Atlanta United soccer game and we elect to take public transportation to neglect downtown traffic. My friends and I arrived at the same train station that my dad and I used to pick my mother up at. The parking lot hasn't changed at all since the late 90's. If I close my eyes, I can almost beam myself back to the time my dad played *Radio Ga Ga* by Queen for the first time while waiting for my mom's train to arrive. My dad wasn't a good singer, but he knew exactly how to imitate Mercury's tenor range and it'd always amuse me. This is also the same train station that led Indah directly to the airport when she left for New York for college. Our entire family woke up at 5 a.m. that morning to load her belongings in the trunk. On the ride to the train station, I silently battled emotions that I'd never felt before. Indah sat in the passenger seat and I sat in the back with my mom and Winny. Indah sensed how quiet I was and would periodically look back and make funny faces to make me laugh—and I wouldn't. I couldn't even make eye contact with her. Every minute that passed was a second closer to saying goodbye and the dread became more and more poignant. Once we arrived, my dad unloaded heavy suitcases one by one while my mother hugged Indah. I couldn't hear what she was saying to Indah, but I'd imagine the exchange was optimistic and assuring. My mom was frightened upon learning that Indah aspired to flee the nest and move to New York City. Of all places, she chose to go to a college that was the farthest from home – and she was adamant. My parents, no matter how hard they tried to discourage her, couldn't convince Indah otherwise. She was the bravest out of all of us. My parents had to accept it. This is, after all, what they brought their family to America for: opportunities. This was Indah's strongest rebuttal. Winny said her farewells, quick and cordial. And then it was my turn. She kneeled down to my eye level and did her best to console me, but nothing worked. The sadness turned into anger. I didn't say a word to her. She hugged me while my arms were crossed, lips pouted. I didn't understand how monumental this move was for her and it was hard to be happy about it. To me, it meant I would never have her around to laugh with ever again. Whenever Mom or Dad upset me, she'd find me sobbing in the closet and worked tirelessly to find anything to stop the crying. Once, our parents sent us both to the Chinese restaurant in the shopping center down the street to pick up our to-go order. While waiting for our food, a customer came in and said, "I'm here to pick up my *pu pu platter*" and I looked over at Indah as we both erupted in convulsive laughter. With Chinese take-out in the backseat, Indah and I took the long way home while Greenday's *Dookie* album blared from the speakers of Dad's car.

My dad pulled the last heavy suitcase out from the trunk and said his goodbyes. We all watched her walk diligently through the entrance of the train station. It was hard to see through the tears. It's strange to think that at one point in our lives, my sisters were painting their nails and watching their favorite episode of *Friends* (the "smelly cat" episode) in the living room. My mom was in the kitchen muddling chili peppers and garlic, and my dad was on the computer doing paperwork. We were all in the house together, occupying space in every room and being each other's company for the very last time - and none of us ever knew it. After everything that our family had gone through together, we'd eventually part ways and start lives of our own. This train station—the only thing resilient and consistent for me—has been a memorial for my family's best and worst times.

On the train heading home from the stadium, my husband stood on his feet and held a straphanger to forfeit his seat for an older Hispanic lady to sit. She seemed tired, dozing off every few minutes, as if she had just gotten off a long shift. I took a moment to ingest everything around me: working class people of different ethnicities to upper-class women with Chanel purses and art students in Doc Martens and drinking pastel-colored boba tea. A young Asian mom sat across from me as her daughter slowly emerged out of deep slumber. She stared directly at me with sleepy eyes. I hoped that she never changes her name or loses the ability to speak her mother's language. I hoped that she'd visit her country more than once and won't hide her culture in cabinets or that the girls in her future high school won't coerce her into going blonde. I wish, more than anything within that moment, that we would leave a nicer world for this girl. I could smell the food that people bought from food trucks which instantly ignited hunger pains. Different fragrances of food filled the train, but I didn't have a taste for any of it: I didn't want hot dogs. Cheeseburgers didn't sound appetizing. I wanted *nasi goreng*. I wanted to slice a fried egg with a fork and watch the yolk melt into the rice. I wanted to bite into a cucumber when the heat became too overpowering. I wanted to come home to the same smells that I'd complain to my mom about. I wanted to find her in my kitchen with all the windows opened, stirring mystery ingredients in a wok.

"Why are you so quiet?" my husband asked.

"Are you hungry?"

"No," I began.

"I'm homesick."

MISS WORLD

There was a strange kind of sadness that overcame me upon realizing that my friendship with Dani was deteriorating. It wasn't the kind of mourning I felt many times before in the past with loss. With sudden deaths or bad breakups, there is forfeiture that's much easier to face with acceptance. With Dani, however, it was harder to let go of her as gracefully.

Dani was a lithe, waifish classmate who sat in front of me in 5th grade. She wore Limited Too shirts that were often so glitzy and loud, that she'd leave behind a trail of sparkly shit on my test papers. Dani being the new girl in our class was exciting because most kids in our grade had known each other for years, so it was the stir of curiosity and fascination that made her popular almost instantly. She had many boyfriends; a few of them were boys in my neighborhood that I grew up with, but for some reason they could never see in me the same charm that they saw in Dani. I suppose this was because, unlike

Dani's feminine allure, I was smelly, burped the ABC's, and wore baggy clothes. I had my heart set on Matthew, a scratchy voiced boy that I shared my first kiss with at the park. Shortly after, I lost his attention once he began the daily regimen of walking Dani home from school. Two weeks later, he showed me the breakup letter that Dani had written him in fuchsia colored jelly ink, informing him that she'd moved on to Angel, a foreign exchange student from Bulgaria. Although Matthew was finally free from her grasp, nothing special ever grew between him and me. It was exceptionally difficult to measure up to Dani. She had the daring fearlessness to let him touch her budding breasts in the gymnasium. As if the pubescent male gaze wasn't enough to sustain her powers, she was also well-liked among the girls. Dani was the first in our grade to menstruate and so it was the strange mixture of envy and obsession that brought her many friends. She had loyal believers that sat around her during lunch. They braided her waist-long, curly, espresso colored hair and passed along Teen Bop magazines. She was Miss World with a glimmering tiara and sash, the girl with the most cake, and I really fucking hated her.

One day, at Leslie Burn's birthday party at an outdated skating rink, I lost my balance when one of my clunky wheels got caught in a small groove in the rink. I fell on the hardwood floor and Dani saw, helped me get back on my feet and asked if I was okay. I was surprised— suspicious— by this act of kindness from a girl who would typically ignore me, but I thanked her as she walked me to the restroom. She ran cold water on a paper towel and cleaned the dirt and popcorn kernels around my scathed, inflamed palms.

"I really like your shirt." she said, pointing at a somber Kurt Cobain on my Nirvana band shirt. I was skeptical to learn that a girl who I believed might have owned the Cheetah Girls soundtrack, could also enjoy the sound of disorderly guitar and the lazy vocal delivery of Kurt. For the remainder of the birthday party, we skipped the cake and presents and opted to sit in the parking lot to talk about music. She told me that her mother was a huge fan of Courtney Love and gave her Hole's *Live Through This* album recently.

"I've always admired you," she said after a long awkward pause.

"I always thought that you hated me, so I never said it. All the guys think you're so cool." She let out a nervous laugh, her cheeks rouged red. Within that moment, I felt so guilty to have harbored so much disdain for her in the past. This girl—a goddess whose feet never touched the ground—secretly had feelings of jealousy for *me*. It was both ironic and surprising.

"We should start a band. An all-girl band," I said. "My dad just gave me a Squier electric guitar for my birthday. You should totally come over and see it."

Her eyes lit up.

"You should come over my house next weekend and bring it." She proposed.
She gave me her number and hugged me as her dad came to pick her up. I remember feeling this warmth in my stomach, an extreme surge of happiness and excitement

that I never felt before. Perhaps it was the unfamiliarity of friendliness with another girl that felt foreign to me. I was used to being friends with boys because it just seemed easier. Boys were always willing to give me a chance and were much less neurotic and judgmental, unlike the girls in our grade. With Dani, however, I was able to resonate with her about things that meant the most to me. It was strange, yet reassuring, to be able to have so much in common with someone. It was a form of intimacy that I hadn't received from anyone else in my life before.

We spent our weekends listening to music, playing dress up with her mom's collection of 90's floral baby doll dresses in front of full-length mirrors. We fought over which band members of Good Charlotte were our boyfriends. Her mom, Mrs. Jennings—a beautiful young mom with pointy eyebrows and full lips—would drop us off at the mall where we would dawdle in stores like Hot Topic. She was so loving to her own daughter, so connected and involved with Dani's interests. Unlike my stoic mother, who disapproved of my music and mostly anything that was foreign and different to her. My mom flagged most things like posters of boys in eyeliner and pentagrams doodled on my Chuck Taylors as dangerous and evil. Dani's home was a safe haven where I could be my most authentic self. There were even some weekends when her mom would surprise Dani and me with tickets to see bands like Good Charlotte and Evanescence. My mom was always so hesitant about me going, but I persisted, assuring her that we'd be chaperoned and looked after. When we weren't attending rock concerts, I would spend the night at Dani's house every weekend. Her mom allowed us to watch movies like *The Craft* on DVD, to which we were inspired to put hexes on boys in our school. There was one instance when a boy named Jeremy in my class scoffed dubiously at the idea of witchcraft. He leaned back in his chair with only the two metal back legs supporting him, I stared at him until he fell backwards, crashing on the ground only inches away from bashing his head open on the edge of a table. He stayed away from me ever since. I thought, *Shit, maybe I really am a witch,* so Dani and I began to dabble into the occult even more. If I possessed these supernatural powers to telepathically bring men to their death, what else am I capable of? We found a Ouija board at a vintage thrift store. It was missing the planchette, so we used a piece of cardboard to call on spirits. We even tried to put a binding spell on a mean girl named Brittany who we nicknamed "Skanky Panky" until she told the teacher on us. I was called into the principal's office. Ms.Ellen, a middle aged plump woman with thick spectacles, asked to see my hands. They were covered in the mantra *"I bind you, Brittany, from doing harm—against others and against yourself."* Because of this, my mom thought that it was irresponsible of Dani's mom to allow children with impressionable minds like ours to see movies about the dark arts, so it became harder to go over Dani's house. This didn't stop us from becoming inseparable, however. On weeknights, we'd sneak on the phone and have hour long conversations until one of our parents would wake up, disconnect the line, and scold one of us to go to bed. Our classmates, even teachers, were taken by surprise at such an unlikely pair.

Through the years, our roots intertwined, and we grew even closer as we experienced the tumultuous horrors of teen angst together. I discovered self-mutilation at thirteen years old, using my father's box cutter from a rusty toolbox in the garage to slice horizontal patterns into my forearms. I covered the scars with terry cloth wristbands from Spencer's that usually said things like *Normal People Scare Me* or black jelly bracelets. For a while, nobody ever suspected a thing. Dani's scars were less difficult to conceal since the cutting was mostly on her thighs.

This was also around the age where we were sexually curious, although I was still shy and modest about boys. There was a group of teenage skater boys who'd congregate at the plaza down the street from my house. It had an abandoned Wendy's and a big empty parking lot. Dani and I would go on walks to get slushees and sit on the sidewalk to ogle at the swoopy-haired sweethearts.

"Oh, *that* one is cute." Dani said, pointing to one of the boys who had taken off his shirt and wore it under his trucker hat to absorb sweat.

"Well, if you claim him, then *he's* mine." I replied, referencing a dirty blonde wearing a System of a Down band t-shirt who also used shoelaces as a belt.

"Wait, no! I totally saw him first!" Dani let out a bellowing laugh, showing off a stained blue tongue.
The dirty blonde must have seen us talk about him because he immediately made eye contact with me and careened toward us on his skateboard. I grabbed Dani's

hand in disbelief. "He's coming over to us!" I whispered as we both let out a muffled squeal. His name was Shane and I fell completely head over heels in love the instant he introduced himself. Dani was chatty, but I remained quiet, resenting my shyness and only laughing at occasional jokes in their interaction. He smiled at me, showing the little gap in his teeth. I romanticized the freckles that the sun brought out on him. He brought us over to his group of friends. They sized us up like vultures, but it wasn't long until we befriended and infiltrated Shane's social circle. We spent hot summer days watching these boys impress us with their skating tricks. We slurped slushees, listened to System of a Down's *Toxicity* album on our iPods, and carved anarchy symbols on buildings, despite not having a full understanding on what it meant.

A few weeks later, Shane asked me if I wanted to lose my virginity to him, suggesting I sneak out that night and meet him somewhere. He placed a sweaty hand on the meatiest part of my thighs.

"Um, I don't know. My mom is a light sleeper." I explained. He paused.

"Well," he began, pointing at a Dunkin Donuts. "We could go into the unisex restroom in there and I could fuck you right now."

My cheeks became hot to the touch. His advances were just not plausible. My mom had terrorized me with the concept of pregnancy the summer before. I bled in my underwear and cried to her, frightened and confused. She had given me an oversized pad and said: "You have to be careful now. Don't hang around boys because you can get pregnant. Do you want to end up like all your sister's friends?" Dani was less fearful, explaining sex as "just skin going into skin" when I confided in her about Shane's proposition. I was always envious of her bravery.

One day, we attended Warped Tour in 2006 with Shane and they held hands together the entire time. It was evident that our competition for his attention was pointless, despite making it clear to her that I was in love with him. On the ride home, I looked over at them and saw Shane fingering her in the backseat behind her dad in the driver's seat. I felt a hot rock sliver down my esophagus and into my stomach that never hit the bottom. She would call me "prude" for teasing boys and I guess, to an extent, she was right. Boys would get frustrated with my reluctance to put out, and my self-consciousness about the fact that I was yet to understand my own sexuality.

One night, my mom caught a glimpse of the scars on my arm. She cried—not out of worry—but out of frustration with not being able to understand or control me. This was around the time when my dad found a job opportunity in Louisiana. She suggested that I move to Baton Rouge with him. Her intention was to remove me from bad influences, particularly Dani, who she believed might have inspired me to self-injure, despite the fact that it was *I* who glamorized it to her. What amused me was how neither of my parents ever asked why I harmed myself. Why weren't they concerned about the emotional and mental disturbance I was feeling that caused me to carve chunks into my limbs like a Thanksgiving turkey?

They were too focused on figuring out the perfect punishment instead of finding the underlying reason for my mania.

By the end of summer, when all my friends who I'd known since childhood started their first year of middle school, I was packed for Baton Rouge to make an entirely new set of friends. I despised my mom for many years for sending me away. I barely spoke to her while I lived in Louisiana. Even when my mom was in a bad car accident back home in Georgia, I never visited her in the hospital. Dani's parents eventually found out about her self-mutilation, too. They sent her off to see a therapist. I lived in Louisiana for two years and lost touch with her after the first year.

By 8th grade, my father was making good money at his job in Louisiana. We were able to afford a big house in a predominately Jewish suburban neighborhood back in Atlanta. By then, my first plan of action was to reconnect with Dani again. We were going to start the last year of middle school in different parts of town, but we promised each other that we would remain friends like we were in our golden days. We tried to defeat the odds. Unfortunately, being exposed to so many new people made it difficult to preserve what was left of our friendship. On occasion, when time would allow, we'd catch up on each other's lives and rekindled our flames over *The Vampire Diaries* on weekends. But nothing was ever the same. There was an impending doom of truth we tried hard to repress; we were growing apart. After only a small amount of time, we stopped talking to each other entirely. By then, I'd only ever keep up with her through social media, scrolling past photos of her with another girl, who seemingly ended up being a much better, and much more fitting, best friend. It seemed ridiculous to own up to this feeling of melancholy, but I couldn't deny the sadness I felt about time replacing me.

Before there were boys, there was a girl I loved in the purest way, and nobody could ever measure up to her. What I didn't know then, was that I was going through textbook heartbreak. It took me until my mid-twenties to realize that Dani could have possibly been my first love. With this knowledge, I went through cycles of confusion. Could I possibly be able to love both men and women? I thought of it in theory and deemed it was possible to be emotionally available to both. For the most part, my love life has always been heteronormative; I've always loved the security and warmth of a man and how they held me like a gem; their sleepy, coaxing voices and heavy hearts. I had visions of a big wedding with a backless, lacy dress, prince charming on a noble steed. 90's Leonardo DiCaprio. John Travolta in *Face/Off*. But the beauty of a woman has always been just as enthralling to me. Men were easy to bewitch, predictable in their nature, yet women captivated me and made me feel coy and nervous. Women are delightfully complex. It's the sense of immersing yourself completely and realizing that there's still another world beneath the trenches. Admiring women has always been easier to do; rose petal soft skin, supple lips, and the poetic way the middle of Dani's spine looked when she put on a bra. At an early age, I was taught to be comfortable with my body around other girls. Seeing Dani naked was normal. On some afternoons, she'd rest her head on my lap as she divulged her frustration about school and boys while I braided her hair. It was the subtle physical connection that brought me closer to her.

Since then, many women have come in and out of my life. I'd become close to them but never like how I was with Dani. In high school, I befriended a beautiful green eyed Venezuelan named Sofia. She had pillowy lips, beautiful teeth, curly hair and a pear-shaped body. I was instantly enamored. We bonded over Gwen Stefani in drama class. Once, she lent me her hardback copy of *Girl, Interrupted* by Susanna Kaysen. We both had a fascination with astrology and Angelina Jolie. During this time, my parents went back to Indonesia for a month. They trusted me to go to school, look after the house, and fend for myself for the time being with their credit card. I invited Sofia over, and we drank my mom's dessert wine and ordered Chinese food. We learned that we were both late bloomers. Our virginity was still intact and we were inexperienced, so we decided to practice making out. It was the first time I'd ever been sexual with a girl. I could taste the sweetness of the dessert wine on her slippery tongue. She climbed on top of me. I put my hands on the curves of her tiny waist. I could feel myself getting wet. She climbed off me and covered her mouth with her hands.

"I can't believe we just did that!" she exclaimed.

We never spoke about it ever again.

One time, another girl named Lynn and I went to the movies to watch *Snakes on A Plane*. It wasn't scary at all, but for some reason it was just scary enough for her to grab my arm and hold my hand. I remember feeling a debilitating sensation in my stomach, so full of adrenaline and *what the fuck-ness*. I realized how badly I was yearning for a woman's physical affection. Gentle grazing or small glimpses of her breast when undressing in front of me sent my head into a flurry.

Elizabeth from drama class often forced me to lie about my whereabouts to my parents so that we could smoke weed at the park. She introduced me to cool indie music and gave me a bunch of mix cd's. I spent nights at her house in Grant Park, a yuppie neighborhood with Victorian-style houses and Craftsman bungalows. Rainbow flags waved on front porches and well-manicured rose bushes entwined white-picket fences. At dusk, we walked along the sidewalk of her neighborhood to smoke joints and we could hear the trumpet sounds from the elephants at the Atlanta Zoo nearby.

Claudia, a senior in my high school, used to pick me up on Friday nights and we'd drink Smirnoff vodka in her basement with cute boys and drive around the neighborhood. I remember rolling the window down and vomiting onto the side of her car while Metallica blared on the radio.

There was Kylie, who came into my life unexpectedly in my early twenties. I would knock on her door at 7 a.m. after a cocaine comedown and she'd tuck me in bed, feed me hummus and watch *The Bachelorette* with me. We weren't necessarily always good for each other, inspiring the worst demons within ourselves during $5 margarita nights, fighting and arguing. But I was in love with our friendship. We kissed each other on the lips regularly. With my eyes, I traced the moles on her neck that looked like constellations and fell in love with the way her nose scrunched up when she laughed.

And then, in my mid-twenties, there was Stella; an aspiring actress who had macchiato eyes that captivated me the moment I met her. She was the hostess at a bar I was working at. She would read books during the slower hours. I worked up the nerve to talk to her by asking if she could write out a list of book recommendations. She scribbled a list of books on a piece of paper with her phone number. Eventually, we spent cold evenings walking along the sidewalks, en route to her favorite donut shop in the cool part of town. We each talked about our plans for our futures with the crisp sound of November leaves collapsing underneath our footsteps. I spent the night at her house once and we watched serial killer documentaries and French films. To bed, she wore only a Calvin Klein bralette and underwear. I was never certain whether or not her friendship with me was only platonic, but I wished to be able to immerse myself in her completely and find out. It was the best example of the right person at the wrong time; she had a boyfriend and I was also in a heterosexual relationship with a man who I truly loved. I said, "Cute underwear!" and went to sleep. By the time summer came around, her boyfriend broke up with her. She went to Italy to find herself. Before she left, she lent me two of her favorite books which, for writers, is probably the deepest form of intimacy. When she came back from Italy, tanned and happy, she told me that she planned to move to New York City. Eventually, she fell in love with a woman and that was that.

One night shortly after my 26th birthday, I received a message from Dani on Facebook.

"Hello" the message said.

It was a ridiculously simple thing to say after many years of estrangement. We spent the next few hours sending messages back and forth until she invited me over to her new home. It was in the newly gentrified part of town and we planned to drink red wine on her couch. The moment she opened the front door, I was greeted with a face that never aged after the night at the skating rink. I told her I wanted to write books. She told me she was in school for makeup.

"I have something to show you!" she exclaimed, gulping a mouthful of wine before slamming the glass on the coffee table and darting to her closet. She came back into the living room with her arms held behind her.

"Are you ready for this?" she asked in a sing song-y voice. She then spread out a big black Nirvana t-shirt which I recognized the more I stared at it.

"That's the t-shirt I wore at Lesley Burn's birthday party at the skating rink." I said under my breath. "Oh my god."

By 3 a.m., we were both tired and dizzy from the wine. It was time to go. Upon parting, she held the door open for me and I wrapped my arms around her tightly and told her to never let years pass us by without seeing each other again. It was the last time I ever saw her.

When I revisit these memories, a part of my heart desperately yearns for what we once had. It took me a long time to understand, but I think about it now and I realize that love is just an organic thing that rebirths and rots. Womanhood entails a constant flux of firsts and lasts and knowing when to accept the process of letting things flow in and out. You can be sad about it—all the precious things that life's fluidity takes, the losses, the warm beings that held you when you felt isolated and scared—but these people don't dissipate or die. They will just live their own lives. You will live yours. Together, you both will own a silent commemoration for these memories. We needed each other in our teen years. That sense of sisterhood was the only way either of us could have survived the limbo between childhood and adulthood. Without it, without this sense of interconnection and understanding, we would have had to face growing pains alone. We knew we were lucky to have someone there to say, "I know exactly what you mean" at the end of each day. Our hearts are often so desperate for anyone to be able to interpret our intensity and, if you're lucky, there will be someone who can fluently articulate our own internal language. We will have them for a while and then we may never have them again. Dani was my first lesson in moving on and differentiating nostalgia from love. It was the first of many things, but above all, she was an ominous dark horse of loss that I'll eventually experience many times again in the future.

ELF ON A SHELF

"We not celebrate Christmas," my dad reiterated in broken English, cooling off a spoonful of corn chowder with gentle blows from his lips. After a quick slurp, he continued: "We are Muslim."

In agreement, my mom would then ask me to take down my makeshift "Christmas tree." It was just an artificial tree with plastic, spiky leaves. They wanted me to strip it of all my handcrafted ornaments—which were made from glitter and papier-mâché at school. The *Welcome Santa* sign was permissible, for whatever reason, but not the plate of macadamia cookies and glass of milk which would have "attracted the ants".

Like most non-Christians, the 25th of December was just another day for us. The most festive thing my mom ever did in my childhood on Christmas day was making a tradition out of eating homemade soup while my dad blared Rod Stewart's 2003 album *As Time Goes By: The Great American Songbook, Vol. II* on his stereo system. None of it made any sense. We just sat in happy silence, burning the roof of our mouths while the sound of melodious saxophone and Stewart's whiskey-soaked voice serenaded us by the fireplace. It wasn't the quintessential look of a Hallmark Christmas, but it was ours.

When the holidays approached, excitement grew in my 1st grade class. Our teacher rolled in a squeaky TV cart and played *How the Grinch Stole Christmas* while we decorated sugar cookies. Those who celebrated Christmas talked amongst themselves about the presents they were expecting from Santa. I remember feeling completely estranged in silence. Even the Jewish kids brought latkes for the class. The ones who celebrated Kwanzaa, wore beautiful intricate dashikis. And what did the Muslim kids get? We had to pick off pepperoni slices off our pizzas because our parents wouldn't let us eat pork.

Sometimes on Christmas Eve my parents would allow me to spend the evening at our neighbor's house, the Kinney's. It filled me with excitement because it was the only time that I would ever see a glimpse of real Christmas. They kept the lights dim in their house, leaving only their massive Christmas tree to illuminate the entire living room. Mrs.Kinney gathered her kids and me around a porcelain nativity scene and told us about Jesus Christ while we slopped icing on gingerbread houses with gumdrop roofs. Afterwards, we would watch *Home Alone* and *Home Alone: Lost in New York*. More importantly, she also kept these plastic elves—with spine-chilling smiles and menacing eyes—around the house. They were wedged between two books on a shelf, above the fireplace, and bedside on nightstands. I once found one in the refrigerator behind the leftovers when I tried to retrieve a glass of milk to drink with my sugar cookies. I saw a white and red striped limb sticking out behind the Tupperware and I gasped in astonishment when I saw an elf peering into my pupils with a macabre smile. I later learned that these were just some of Santa's helpers sent from the North Pole to watch children by day, to report back to Santa with who's been naughty or nice. The entire thing felt intrusive and sinister.

Mrs.Kinney also showed us how to make *real* snowmen—made with carrots and plastic buttons. They were different from the ones my family made. The snowmen my sisters and I built on our first snow day in our first year living in the United States had bok choy noses. It was December 1994 and our family had never seen snow before. Most of the people living in our sleepy apartment complex were snuggled up tightly in their warm homes, but we spent the majority of the morning scraping the snow off of Dad's car and throwing it at each other, fascinated by the beauty of white layers of frozen ice crystals. The 35mm photos that my mom took with her single-use camera show my dad wrapping his arms around my sisters and me, smiling, bundled in flannel and peeking through oversized beanie hats with wobbly pom-poms.

During a few times out of the year, my parents pulled us out of class to visit *masjid*, which was a place of worship for Muslims. We had to wear long white tunics and a hijab that covered our heads (but not our faces) and pray on prayer rugs that had intricate designs. My mom nudged me in the arm whenever I'd forget to greet strangers with *"salaam alaikum."*. Even as a child I knew that the entire thing felt uneasy. I didn't know much about religion (or really anything for that matter) yet, somehow, I was still self-aware enough to understand that I did not belong there. My parents never told me about the importance of our Islamic faith but showing up and taking it seriously was something my sisters and I knew we had to do. None of us ever questioned whether we believed in it. I think, for the most part, we were just unwilling to argue with Mom about religion. The only benefit to any of this was my parents taking us to Taco Bell afterwards. I'd get soda in a cup with Uma Thurman as Poison Ivy for a promotional advertisement for the 1997 film *Batman & Robin*.

When four unsmiling terrorists drove an airplane into the World Trade Center in 2001, we stopped going to masjid. My parents decided it was safer to keep their religious beliefs as inconspicuous as possible. It seemed more sensible to. In a neighborhood that was predominantly old, white, and conservative, my parents didn't want to face any more scrutiny. My dad shaved his thick, black goatee and my mom wore the hijab sparingly until not at all. There was a tire swing at an abandoned house a few blocks from our house that kids in my neighborhood would often trespass and congregate at. The GoodYear tire hung from a dirty rope wrapped around a flexible limb of an old Red Oak tree. I was next to have a turn on the tire swing when a boy named Tyler called me *Osama Bin Laden's daughter*. I went home that day feeling dejected.

As my sisters and I grew older, my parents loosened the reigns and allowed us to decide what religion was right for us. Suddenly, at 15, I was on the market for a God. Is my God omnipresent, hovering above me in a white robe? Was it even a man? I liked the idea of an ethnically ambiguous woman as my God. She wore loose silk that exposed a heavy breast, had curls in her hair and smelled like cherry blossoms. I imagined angels playing the harp for her and grapes being fed to her by strong, chiseled men. As an angsty teenager, apathy was a reflective reaction towards religion for me. I felt like if God was real then He or She wouldn't have allowed my dog to die or given the girls in my school B-cup breasts while I was flat as a board. What God is this unfair? Every slight inconvenience in my teenage life was a cruel joke made by an even crueler God. That was the age I discovered Marilyn Manson and thought I was at the forefront of an edgy trend for carving pentagrams on wooden desks at school.

In high school, I dated a Christian guy whose family owned a mega church. I would come to a few morning services and watch his mother socialize with churchgoers and friends. I didn't mind the fellowship. I liked the ideology behind their faith and the sense of community: for all to assemble under one roof for the same reasons. His mother was beautiful and reminded me of Jamie Lee Curtis in *True Lies*—she had beautiful silver hair that was brushed back and always wore statement heels to church. Most people would assume Christian women in the south were intolerant and judgmental, especially about my religious background, but she was always so kind and loving to everyone. Afterwards we'd all eat an early lunch at Cracker Barrel and I'd watch his Grandfather, the Pastor of the church, cut his country fried steak into small squares and share stories from his childhood. *I could do this*, I thought. I could see myself dedicating Sundays to talk about the Gospel and eat mashed potatoes mixed with buttered corn. I thought maybe Christianity might work, but I wasn't able to commit just yet.

In my early twenties, however, I was no longer concerned about searching for the perfect God. My main focus was falling in love with atheist boys who fed my cynicism. I dated the kind of metalhead that thought writing *666* on his sneakers was a personality trait. He was a drummer of a thrash metal band and would often yell "Hail Satan!" during inappropriate times and thought it was clever. Anytime we'd go to house parties or chug Pabst Blue Ribbons at metal shows, he'd take it upon himself to showcase his disdain for the Catholic church in casual conversation unrelated to denomination.

My fascination with metaphysics and spirituality first started when a friend of mine, a red headed art student named Heidi, and I smoked weed in her parent's basement. What was interesting about Heidi was how although she was never religious, she still possessed a strong sense of purpose and certainty in life without the indoctrination of a religion. I admired this about her. She wasn't lost and directionless like I was. She was so wise, an Oracle of some sort, a strong feminine force that was inspiring to be around. I always wished her light absorbed some of my darkness and shed onto me. She passed me a poorly rolled joint, flimsy, with residue collecting at the mouthpiece which transferred gunk onto my lips.

"There's a full moon tonight," she began.

I maintained eye contact with Heidi, confused with how to answer.

"Yeah."

"And you know what I haven't done in a while?"

Before I could say anything, she hopped off the bed and dug through cabinets. She pulled out a wooden box and brought it back to the bed where I laid, stoned and confused.

"Let's do a tarot reading."

The ends of her lips curl up into a smile.

My eyes widened.

She brought out a porcelain vintage tea set and we drank licorice tea as Nag Champa filled the room with an air of mystique. We sat on the cold floor as she brought over her altar (it was just a breakfast tray with a mandala painted on it, something she'd refer to as "sacred geometry" or something) decorated with an assortment of crystals and sage. She pulled out a deck of cards. She brought out a chunk of wood and set the tip on fire with a lighter, the cherry burning and releasing ribbons of smoke that smelled like sweet pine and mint. She recognized the curiosity in my face.

"This is called Palo Santo wood," she explained.

"It's been used for healing and good fortune by shamans for centuries." She wafted the piece of wood, now on fire, in circular motions as she slowly moved around the entire room. She set it down on an ashtray and picked up a deck of tarot cards.

"Close your eyes. Shuffle through these cards and think of any questions you want answered or any issues you have that you want clarity to."

"How long do I shuffle?" I asked, blindly intermixing cards together.

"*Shhh*, as long as you feel like you should. Until you think it's ready."

I shuffled for fifteen more seconds and placed the deck of cards faced down. Within those fifteen seconds, my mind focused on the last three years: I'd been in a long-term relationship with someone who was bad for me and I couldn't get out. I dropped out of school for the third time. I needed answers to questions that I'd been neglecting to ask myself, let alone out loud to the cosmos.

"Okay, now pick a card from this deck and place it in the middle of the altar."

I picked the first card on the top of the deck and flipped it over. It seemed ominous and frightening at first, a feminine figure with the face of a cartoon moon, lovelorn on a balcony with her hand on her chin, bored. I noticed that a cup was falling from her grasp. In a booklet, she reads out its meaning:

Four of Cups

Depression, a feeling of worthlessness, withdrawal. You may have suffered a string of disappointments and feel the need to hide away from the world.

I glared at Heidi in astonishment as if the cosmos reached its hands into the deepest crevices and pulled out the rot for me to examine in the light.

"Okay, but like, how did it know that?" I demanded to know. She smiled and tilted her head in a way that said *told you.* She decided to give me the deck of cards as a gift and since then, I gave myself a reading at every full or new moon. I would even keep it in my purse so that, at parties, I could take it out and offer free readings to drunk girls.

From then on, I felt like I finally found my perfect theology. I found a metaphysical store on the other side of town that had cats sunbathing on windowsills. There were wind chimes hanging on trees that tinkled even when there was no wind, a fountain that gurgled, and world music on low volume that made me feel like I was in J.R.R Tolkien's Middle-earth. Everything smelled like patchouli. Calmness overcame me, my shoulders dropped, and time became just an illusion. I read books about the paranormal and astrology, sitting Indian style in the aisle and shifting through pages. I made my way to the crystals which were in glass bins that displayed their names and their healing properties. I picked up a smooth blue crystal with wispy white patterns that looked like cirrus clouds moving across a blue sky:

AGATE

Detoxifies

Eases Anxiety

A Cold Agate Used On The Forehead Is Generally Effective In Curing Fever

Oh, I thought out loud. The natural next step is to demonstrate on myself. I held the crystal onto my forehead with my index finger just as a sales associate restocked the amethyst crystals beside me.

"C-can I help you?" she asked, sweetly with a tiny bit of condescension.

"No, just looking around. Thank you." The agate is still intact. I *did* notice how I was feeling this newfound sense of peace. I wasn't sure if this was magic or mental. There I was, rummaging through a witch shop petting Calico cats and sticking rocks on my face. This prompts me to ask myself an important question: What the fuck is the difference between this and actual religion? Why am I more willing to accept the healing properties of sticks and stones but not faith or worship towards someone in the sky? I have no idea why it's hard for me to accept the God formula; the belief that if you pray and serve one God was ludicrous and I couldn't accept it. But these crystals, these shops, gave me a piece of mind and serenity. I've visited chapels and old churches in Italy and remembered how ominous and sanctified everything felt. I felt like I didn't belong, scared and displaced. But with Wiccan, I felt okay. A psychology student once told me that dreams are just our brain's way of naturally creating stories while also getting rid of excess information it doesn't need. Often when I am unconsciously hallucinating, I re-visit the exact same places in my dream world. A popular one is a desolate meadow during what seems to be like early spring; the wheat colored grass moves with the wind, the ominous grey clouds hurry across the sky, and even the smell of rain is poignant. This would usually sound serene and tranquil, but the confusion and solitude of being alone in an empty space becomes rather uncomfortable and frightening. I also have dreams of coming to the same train station, which I hate too. It is never certain what my destination is, yet there is a thud in my chest that tells me I'm not going in the right direction. I am stuck feeling helpless and lost, either getting in the wrong train or not making it in time for the right one. Ironically, the ones that I don't mind are the vivid ones where I am bound— by barnacles—onto a dead whale. Together, my 100,000-pound friend and I are sinking into the ocean's deep trenches where no light can reach, and the rotting corpse and I are being eaten alive by eels. Strangely, it's so morbidly beautiful.

The worst dreams, which come more often than the rest, are of my teeth: dreams of my teeth crumbling in my mouth like broken seashells, spitting it out to no avail as more and more teeth keep falling out. With these dreams I'd wake up in panic and touch every tooth with my tongue to make sure all were still intact. But the notion that there might not be any significance to these dreams is ugly and boring, therefore it's a reality I choose not to accept. I am beginning to suspect that this is *exactly* what I do with metaphysics. Maybe creating your own system of faith and worship is, at its core, the same as anything else. I've come across skeptics who would scoff at my tarot card readings that I insisted on giving.

"Jen, these cards are all so ambiguous and vague. It's easy for anyone to find any meaning that pertains to their life. It's all bullshit."

"Well, sure," I began to rebut. "But there's a reason why you picked these. Out of allll the cards you could have picked, you picked these. Don't you think that counts for something?"

"No, also please stop bringing sage into my house."

I once gave myself a tarot card reading in front of one of my ex-boyfriends. At the time, I suspected he'd been cheating on me, but he was excellent at gaslighting women, so my paranoia was negated. I hid my suspicion and acted like I didn't know. He laid on his side, holding his head up with his hand while I sat on the floor with my cards spread out. I picked the first card:

Two of Cups:

You are attracted to someone wholly unsuitable.
Enter into any long-term
commitment with eyes wide open. The end of this
relationship is well overdue

We were so tense with discomfort, neither of us breathed for the entirety of fourteen seconds. Breaking the silence, he sat up, inhaled, exhaled. He reached over and scrambled the cards out of place before saying: "Alright, enough of this. Let's not do this." A month later, I found out he was seeing his ex-girlfriend the entire time. This might have been the most obvious and clear affirmation with tarot I'd ever gotten, almost too self-evident but, nonetheless, tarot had a way of giving subtle nods. It was a way to communicate to whatever was out there that always had my back. I mean, how could there *not* be a natural semblance to things? A Wiccan lady held my hand once at my husband's family gathering and told me that, upon meeting me for the first time, she could sense a regal female in either my past life or within my bloodline. She had visions of a beautiful queen with roses by her feet. Everyone loved her. Years later, I mentioned this to my mom. That's when I first learned that four generations ago in the island of Java, a king from the city of Surakarta went to the village to pick out a lover.

"And the lover he chose ended up being your great great great great grandmother. You *do* have something special in your bloodline, even if it's just a tiny drop." she explained.

I think of how many times I day I escape from death's grip without my knowledge and come to realize that my ancestors must be protecting me.

Alienation has always been a huge part of my childhood. I've felt like Christianity was something I was never invited to. But spirituality was always there, waiting for me whenever I was impatient and confused. These overpriced rocks, these cards, all of it: if it's a scam, a way to get money out of people's emotions, what made real religion any different?

We spend our lives seeking a formula that gives us a summation for perfect answers: Does God really take young children from us by giving them cancer because he needs more angels in heaven? Is it actually necessary for koalas in Australia to be barbequed to a crisp in wildfires? When a sick, elderly man leaves the same world that a baby has just been born into, is this balance? I make an illegal left turn and barely miss a speeding Porsche, and I am convinced that my ancestors made a deal with Death to buy me more time. We use things like religion, science, metaphysics, and spirituality to help us piece things together, choosing only the parts we like. And none of us are right or wrong.

Choosing to believe in a natural semblance of things has kept me sane. It's kept me patient during the hard times. We try to reason with a universe that operates with no fixed plan, a universe that takes and gives whenever it wants despite our feelings and attitude towards it. We take our frustrations and reason with it instead; try to find sense in unsystematic chaos. And if our answers are wrong and there's truly darkness and only nothingness in the end for us all in the next life, at least the belief that there is more has kept me alive long enough for this one.

BAD SKIN

I think about death a lot for someone who cares about which cereal will help them live the longest. One serving of regular whole grain oat Cheerios is 100 calories. 150 if you add in ½ cup of skim milk. 1g of sugar. 20g of carbs. In terms of food, particularly in the context of caloric intake, there is euphoria in numbers that high school calculus never gave me. My theory is that managing how much I eat gives me a sense of control where I might lack in some other aspect. Of course, it's only exactly that: an illusion of control. There are still many other internal issues that are not under any sort of control whatsoever, all of which I am too afraid to reach in the ether and pull out into the light. Somehow, controlling what I eat is just easier. And somehow, those problems disappear here in aisle five: because here in this moment in a gluten-free realm, surrounded by rolled oats and buckwheat, I feel celestial.

As an American, the idea of fad diets (or 45 million Americans dieting in general) is somewhat mocking and satirical to me. It feels wrong that food is so promptly available to us that we have to literally micromanage our gluttony, otherwise we would just kill ourselves from the inside. When we stop to consider things like famine in other parts of the world, I feel like a nincompoop when I scrape the last bite of food on my plate into the garbage as a practice of self-control. I constantly feel like I should be punished for eating out of boredom. Using food as a bonding experience with friends seems unjust. My relationship with food is both paradoxical and erratic but it isn't unlike my relationship with anything else; I am either gluttonous or starving. In love, I am either manically using someone to satiate a hole or willing to deprive myself completely of that person when things go awry. I am a woman of many extremes. When I am sad, I will trick my mind into thinking otherwise by filling my stomach with anything fried and comforting. My favorite in particular is eating ricotta cheese, eating it directly out of the 15 oz. tub. Another thing is southern fried chicken and pairing it with sugary breakfast food. Most of the time, it works. It works, until a year has passed and a staggering 26 pounds has distributed itself throughout my body. Then at that point, I'll most likely wake up one morning and become so engulfed in panic and shame that I begin to neurotically count every calorie and burn double the amount in cardio. Being sedentary after a meal makes me nervous; I always find a way to burn calories. I once used the dog as an excuse to walk around the neighborhood. It's one bowl of Cheerios at noon, another one later in the afternoon, and then a kale salad with no dressing at 6 pm. I won't eat after that. Come morning, my stomach will become flat after the 16-hour fast.

My first experience with weight loss was when I visited Indonesia with my mother when I was 12 years old. I drank the water and ate ill-prepared street food that caused me to be really sick for the entirety of the trip. Along with throwing up all my food and shitting out half my weight, my mother decided to get my dental work done. It would have been cheaper there in Indonesia than it would be in the States. With all the pain medication from two root canals that caused me to feel nauseous, as well my body's inability to nourish itself, eating was very difficult. I began the trip at 95 pounds and by the end of it, I lost nearly 10 pounds in the month we were there. When we returned home, my father was waiting in the terminal for us and was horrified at how frail my body was. He blamed my mother for not taking care of me as well as she should have, even though she *did* try her hardest to put anything in my body that wouldn't find its way back out through my ass. The panic and stress from my sudden weight loss caused my parents to force me to regain health back at home, feeding me rice and protein. I wasn't allowed to go to bed until I finished a glass of whole milk. It took some time, but eventually my body recovered to a healthy point again.

My first experience with weight *gain* was a few years after this, amid puberty. I grew tits over the course of one summer and my body was demanding my ovaries to produce a lot of estrogen, which lead to weight gain. Along with this, the hormonal changes caused my skin to break out mercilessly. I had severe acne that looked like rocky terrain on my forehead and cystic acne on my cheeks— pus-filled nodules that moved whenever I'd smile. My mom would usually blame my skin texture on how "dirty" I was or how I didn't wash my pillow covers enough, even though a dermatologist told us many times that this is a hormonal issue that every normal pre-teen experiences. My mom's skin was pale and as smooth as porcelain, always finding shadow refuge under umbrellas or sunhats on hot days. Her vanity was full of expensive creams and potions due to her elaborate skin regimen. I even remember not being able to kiss her goodnight without my lips accidentally touching the $80 goo on her face. I think her disdain for bad skin made me begin to realize that there are sociocultural ramifications with skin. One might argue that it's classist to assume that everyone has the finances to afford skin care and dermabrasions. How can skin be either "bad" or "good" and how often do we ridicule the person under it? We take things like weight and bad skin, things that have a lot to do with genetics, and make incorrect interpretation that these are signs of someone not taking care of themselves.

One person who never had these problems was my best friend at the time, Danielle. She was a tall brunette, lithe and nimble, with perfect baby skin. We met in a summer program at the YMCA and both liked a boy who went by the name of Fuzzy. He was incredibly hyper-sexual for a 14-year-old. He liked us both. On the bus heading to a water park, he sat between Danielle and me with each of his hands in between our thighs. Later that evening when

I was getting ready for bed, Danielle called me to let me know that they were officially dating. She also made sure I understood that he didn't see me as a good candidate because he noticed how "fat" my thighs looked as they were squished together whenever I sat down. That was his thinking process for choosing a suitable mate. They had sex in the lazy river and got kicked out of the summer camp. I never spoke to them again.

When I made the Cheer Squad for basketball season in 8th grade, I spent two hours practicing every day after school and then ran on the treadmill for an hour at home after that. The Cheer Captain, Kiara, a biracial popular girl who had strong legs, rock hard abs, and a firm peach butt that all the boys praised, inspired me to work hard to have a body like hers. I became addicted to exercising and ate only a banana at lunch. When I thought I was doing a good enough job to reward myself to one cup of my mom's broccoli and cheddar soup, my aunt happened to be in the kitchen. She told me I was gaining weight. She gripped the pinchable fat on my triceps and let out a courtesy laugh. My sister, Indah, lost weight while living in New York City and she looked as chic as her idol, Kate Moss. She was in town to visit and saw me in the kitchen eating the soup. She wiggled her finger and told me, "A moment on the lips, a lifetime on the hips." I'll always remember how the panic struck me immediately; first the anger and then the melancholy. Before the soup digested, I vomited into the toilet bowl upstairs and watched the broccoli florets swim in the pool of bile through watery eyes with the soreness in my esophagus.

In some measure, my eating habits became worse when I reached my twenties, yet—somehow—my body did not reflect it. I finally had the 24-inch waist that Christina Aguilera and Britney Spears had in the early 2000's and gangly limbs. By the time I was 20, I finally had my dream body despite being constantly drunk and spending whatever money I had on liters of Jack Daniels and grams of dive bar cocaine for my ex-boyfriend. I only ever ate during my comedowns from drugs. I worked 12-hour shifts at a Tex-Mex restaurant on 4 hours of sleep. For whatever self-righteous reason, the restaurant hired recovering addicts which worked to my benefit. Access to drugs was easy, with stimulants and depressants constantly at my fingertips. Despite eating empty calories, drinking poison, and depriving myself of sleep, I was the skinniest I'd ever been in my adulthood. All it took to get the body of my dreams wasn't hours of cardio or cheer conditioning—it was self-hate, which was a lot easier.

Viewed retrospectively, it just seems completely unfair as a 27-year-old who's now putting spinach and kale in a blender for dinner to get that body back. Being happy and in love later in life gave me the opportunity to not see food as numbers, which in turn allowed me to not *care* about being skinny. I was able to enjoy food as one of life's simple pleasures, something I'd never viewed food as before. It was no longer the nemesis. I don't feel the need to ask the waiter to serve my fish tacos without the corn tortillas or order a salad at fast food chains and ask the employee to drop one single fry in the bag. I think about how many Thanksgiving dinners I've spent depriving myself of mashed potatoes; picking only at two slices of turkey meat (with no gravy, of course) and roasted carrots, while silently watching in astonishment at how happy and free everybody else was. Nobody seems to care about where the mashed potatoes might distribute visceral fat in their bodies. Everyone just passes the candied yams around and indulge carbohydrates without soul-crushing guilt.

I concede that healing is a long-term process that entails plateaus and failure ahead. It will take time to unlearn what food has always meant to me. On some days, it will always feel like poison in my mouth. On other days, it is escapism from everything that lies in the void within me. It will take me a while to understand that a bathroom is a place to practice self-care and not a place to wage war on myself. It will take me even longer to view food as the necessary means to survive and learn how to establish enough discipline to distinguish pleasure from business. Above all, it takes enough self-love to see the purpose of food as what it really is in actuality: nourishment.

We have hands that feel, legs that carry us to one place to another, and a beating heart: things that our body naturally gives us and still ask nothing from us— except for gratitude.

BAR FRUIT

I've focused too much on how to emerge from the darkness that I'm tempted to stick my hand in it again. Like every annoying, self-absorbed person likes to proclaim, I used to feel everything so intensely: both happiness and sadness gave me equally debilitating sensations. It might have just been hormonal, but at some point as an adult, I felt like it was my responsibility to find healthier ways to control these emotional responses. After years of pinning positive affirmations on Pinterest and reading Eckhart Tolle books, my mind has been conditioned to reflexively battle negative emotions with positive ones. This might sound ideal—however, as a consequence, I sometimes find myself unsure of how to manage ugly feelings whenever I finally *have* to experience them.

One feeling in particular that I have trouble managing is having sentimental longing for things that have already passed. There are certain memories that, due to time in physics, I won't be able to experience ever again because these specific events could only exist once. They've become intangible to me now. I'll never be able to find out what song was playing in the car when I had my first kiss (he dabbled with psychedelics a lot and wore a ponytail so I'm assuming it was anything from *Abbey Road* by the Beatles) or what the weather was like when my friends and I drank vodka from a Gatorade bottle at every high school football game. I won't ever be able to recollect the moments that led to waking up in a hotel bathtub full of cold water during *that one* spring break in Florida. My friend Lynne and I drank Jagerbombs with boys we met at the hot tub and invited them over to our penthouse. They were from London and one of them called me a *crumpet* as a term of endearment. I remember laughing at how dumb it sounded. I swigged Jagerbombs to the face with them, back to back for two hours. I don't remember anything after that. Submerged in a cold bath, I woke up to Lynne's mom shaking me, fearful that I might've needed to go to the emergency room to get my stomach pumped. The boys were nowhere to be found. No matter how hard I try to find the missing piece, nothing can connect the dots. What happened in the moments in between? What happened to my unconscious body before it was dropped off at the hands of a parental guardian? My curiosity for tiny details seeks the answers to so many questions that keep me up at night. This sort of sentimentality has always been so painful. We are often too busy living in important moments that we miss the individual features that create them, and the idea that I'll never be able to astral project into any time period I desire is one that is hard to accept.

One way to trigger this suffering is by logging onto Facebook. For this reason, I try to set fair rules on my internet usage. Like most young women in their late twenties have done, I once miscalculated my time on the internet and found myself in a dangerous domain on Facebook called *Memories*. This new feature provokes you with photos you've forgotten about and invites you to indulge even more: *Don't remember posting this political article last year? Then you definitely won't remember these photos of you from a dive bar that your friends took during 2014's depressive episode. Let's have a look.* I weaved through old photo albums and examined the version of me who hadn't experienced heartbreak yet. Sometimes I grow envious for that sense of purity, the vibrancy of my spirit before men stole years from my youth. Naiveté looked good on me: a lack of experience with real life made me look happier, more optimistic. I saw pictures of a version of me during my slut stage and I wanted to hold her in an empathetic, maternal way. Her hair was long and tousled; she showed her midriff a lot and wanted to be friends with everyone. She had an oversized septum piercing that grazed the top of her lip. I'd like to tell her that things will get better, but I fear I would be lying. I want to tell younger me that the hot mortuary science graduate she hooked up with one summer ended up being a dick, and that he'd end up being a Trump supporter in 2016. I'd tell her that when he said he was too busy to hangout, he was lying. I'd tell her that when he said, "You're pretty hot for an Asian chick", it wasn't a real compliment.

The first time I dropped out of college, I befriended a new group of people who all lived together in a house in the eastside. None of them had parents or a support system to help them financially, so the only people they could really depend on were each other. I found it admirable that their loyalty to one another was a rebellious act against their own resentment for their families. If they couldn't be loved by them, there were other people in the same situation who were willing to provide them with consistency and acceptance. They stole beer kegs and used them for house parties that they charged people to attend to, and these parties became so unexpectedly massive and successful, that this became an effective way to pay their rent. They were, in essence, professional anarchists and the house became a shelter for the misguided. I had parents who loved me and a weekly allowance. For most of my life, I was living with my parents in our 5-bedroom, 3.5 bathroom house in a rich, predominantly Jewish neighborhood. We had a sunroom with marble floors and a backyard the size of a football field. I never starved a day in my life and I had resources for anything available at my fingertips. None of my friends understood why I found common interest with a bunch of punks from the eastside of Atlanta. I was spoiled rotten, sure, but as privileged as I was, I still felt alienated from my own family. At the very least, this was something I had in common with my new friends. My two older sisters moved on with their lives to start their own families, leaving me with only my two neurotic parents who I deeply resented at the time. I left the house as often as I could. Solidifying a bond with hedonists and alcoholics, I found my kinfolk.

At these parties, a metal band played live music in the garage and people fucked in the pool. Consistently, at least six or seven people crammed in a bathroom at once to do cocaine off a dirty sink. Girls from a different side of town came with their own alcohol (usually Malibu rum), took their tops off and danced on top of the kitchen counter. The boys shouted in encouragement while their girlfriends jeered with rude remarks or stared daggers. The front and back yard were overcrowded with people and to park you'd have to circle the block for ten minutes to find an empty space, since the entire neighborhood was lined up with cars. The house buzzed with the loud murmur of a hundred different conversations, music so loud that the reverberation would rattle the windows, and the *tsssst* sound of bottle caps opening. I watched a group of people huddle around a foldable table and played what seemed like hours of beer pong and we noticed how one girl sitting in a chair was nodding in and out of consciousness. She finally dozed off with her head titled back, mouth open. We all kind of found amusement in it until we looked at each other like *Yo, is she okay?* and then, finally, we learned that she was just strung out on heroin after someone found a needle in the bathroom. By morning, the sunlight spilled through the tall windows like a sacred church for the delinquents.

One of the fondest memories I have with these people, is the time we dragged a full keg of Bud Light down to the

Chattahoochee River. Carrying 160 pounds of liquid and metal down a steep hill was only bearable to do when we were already hammered. It was during the time of year in Georgia when caterpillars form nests on the ends of tree branches like spindled gossamer, and the humidity feels gaseous enough to be steeped in. When we found the perfect place to set up camp, we offered beer to strangers and made even more friends. I think people were enamored by our friendship. Our jovial demeanor was magnetic and pure, and the more the merrier. Once the keg kicked and we were left with no more booze, we submerged our drunken bodies in the shit river. We floated down for six hours. This is what Georgians refer to as "shooting the hooch", a recreational activity made popular by our Patron saint, country star Alan Jackson. As we floated down the river, there was a constant swing back and forth between chatty dialogue and the quiet stillness of the water. When the water was at its most tranquil, you could only hear the hoot and chirp of birds. We'd stop to cliff dive which put tremendous stress on our bodies. We'd plunge from twenty-five feet above the water and we'd be so drunk, we'd forget how to do this and just belly flop onto the surface of the water. It was all incredibly dangerous. The most important thing to know before jumping off of this cliff is that there were sharp rocks at the bottom of the shallow end, so it was imperative to back up a few steps and give yourself a head start and jump as far as you could into the deepest part of the water where there were no rocks. There was one kid who didn't get this bit of helpful information: standing over the edge, the fear of heights got to him and he hesitated, which made him accidentally slip off the cliff. He fell straight into the sharp rocks. There was pin drop silence. When his body surfaced, his face was ghost white, but he somehow swam to the shore despite his body being in complete shock. He turned around and streams of blood leaked from the back of his head and down his shoulders. There was an audible gasp. One of my friends swam him to the other side of the river on his back where we tied a t-shirt on his head and called an ambulance.

By late afternoon, raindrops hit the water one droplet at a time until it began to pour. We were freezing, waiting for the rain to pass, huddled under a tree that had branches that gave us a little refuge from the rain. I watched a girl make out with my guy friend and they eventually fucked in the bushes. When the rain stopped, we were all exhausted and hungry. On the car ride home, I hung my arm out of the window as my hand sliced through the warm gusts of wind. I could already feel a cosmic shift in the air. Change was going to happen. We were all quiet on the ride home as if we knew we were just stalling time before having to eventually find more productive ways to spend our summers.

Georgia highways had a way of making time stand completely still. Crooked dents intermittently appear on guardrails as an ominous aftermath of drunk driving. For endless miles, we are confined to a highway that was decorated with religious billboards, ivy-wrapped pine trees, roadside memorials, and kudzu leaves. This was the only purgatory that we knew.

I felt the most beautiful in this directionless stage of my life. I slept with a heavily tattooed mortician and almost fell in love until I started my period mid-coitus and bled on his bed sheets. We kept it platonic after that until we never spoke again. After him, I caught the attention of a musician and found myself cutting the line at every nightclub in Atlanta. I'd find myself chasing tequila with warm orange juice under a DJ booth on a Tuesday night. I was a sparkly trophy, spit-shined on display for his friends. Cocaine made his heart flutter so fast; I'd notice his chest rising and falling and sometimes it worried me. We dated briefly for about three months until I found out he was cheating on me. It had all the merit to send me deeper into a spiraling depression, but I pretended like I didn't know and fucked someone else instead. That was a way for me to feel in control. *You cut me, I stab you.* Cheating felt dangerously good. It was a very strange thing that I was non-expectantly good at. It was a way for me to twist the knife. Why shouldn't I? Men have been ungrateful for the love I've endlessly given them, so the least I could do was reverse the roles and be the one to inflict the pain. *Checkmate.*

A girl named Emily and I were both in shitty relationships at the time and the only way we got through them was by popping two or three Xanax before heading to a strip of bars on the eastside. I'd drink White Russians and boys would say, "Oh, who are you? The Big Lebowski?" and I'd giggle at this joke but never admit that I'd never even seen the movie. To get a bartender's attention when the establishment was packed, I'd lean over and put my tits on the bar, grab a cherry or orange slice from their station and suck on bar fruits with full eye contact until they surrendered their attention to me. It was almost as if my confidence gave me goddess-like energy and I knew harnessing it correctly could tantalize people right into my spider web. Emily's go-to drink was vodka and cranberry. Her eyes glazed whenever she reached the point where she'd become quiet and sad. I was the opposite: I was on every stage singing Stevie Nicks songs on karaoke nights, with my eyes red and cheeks hot, swaying on the dance floor with other sweaty bodies. I was the fun drunk. I'd urge Emily to get out of the funk and dance with me. By the morning, we'd wake up in her bed, unsure of how we arrived home safely, but we depended on that luck to do it all over again. The club would then upload pictures from the night before and we'd laugh and scream whenever a picture of us appeared on our timelines, amused at how neither of us could remember when the photo was being taken. The entire friendship was a cry for help.

All of us knew that, at some point, it was only a matter of time before things had to change. Everyone lost contact as a consequence of growing up. We had jobs to keep. Our survival depended on them. Some people went off to start families of their own, some deemed the city as toxic to their wellbeing and moved to Colorado or California to "find themselves". As most of us reached the end of our twenties, we lost contact almost completely. In our younger years, the iPhone wasn't as accessible as they are now—the only documentation that exists of this time period is poor quality photos taken from old flip phones and videos taken with old digital cameras with shitty resolution. I skimmed through photos and tried to identify faces, playing a silent game called "Whatever Happened to These People?" and came up with my own conclusions about where life might have taken them: *This girl went to rehab, this guy is probably in jail. Yikes, Colorado hasn't been good to this guy. I wonder how long this girl will stay in California until Los Angeles spits her back out. Wait, why does this person look so familiar? Oh yeah, she crashed on my couch for a solid two weeks once. I hope she's doing okay.*

Our faces, smiling candidly or making deliberate vulgar faces with offensive hand gestures, all have a look of blissful, happy ignorance. None of us knew (or cared to know) where fate would bring us to. We all believed we were invincible—to drugs, to drunk driving, and to consequences.

We were blissfully ignorant of how many times we unknowingly cheated death or prison. I'm not necessarily yearning for such pleasure-seeking indulgence anymore and I don't regret what I've outgrown. Surrendering boredom for stability has kept me sane. I'm happy to immerse myself in these photos whenever I come across them. It's like I get to relive the sweetest part of a memory without having to experience the bad parts. I've learned to let the feelings come and go as they please and how to admire them from a different dimension.

Whenever I feel nostalgic about certain events, I'm being taught a lesson on how to distinguish memory from reality: are things as magical as they once seemed or does my mind glamorize the things I'll never have again?

My curiosity peaks.

And I log off.

If there's anything I've learned in life, it's knowing exactly when to log off. Nothing good ever comes from being too curious on the internet.

SPACE COWGIRL

I don't belong here, I thought. There are many places where I know I don't belong, but this is at the top of the list. These were my initial thoughts during a brief pilgrimage to Hampton, Georgia; a bucolic town located forty-five minutes outside of metro Atlanta. It's the kind of Southern neck-of-the-woods where going to Walmart would be considered, at best, doing something somewhat recreational and entertaining. That is, until September arrived.

In the late ripening of autumn, the Atlanta Motor Speedway becomes the home of Imagine Music Festival. It's an annual electronic dance music festival that serves as a massive dancefloor mecca for over 30,000 avid festivalgoers. They gather and frolic freely for two entire days. Initially, it felt morally unjust of me to somehow acquire free tickets to something I would not otherwise ever be interested in. I mean, I liked Billy Joel. If I could curate a playlist for a road trip, it would interchangeably consist of the entire discography of Phil Collins and Peter Gabriel. Whatever a middle-aged, wealthy stepfather would elect to play on his yacht or Porsche, is what would most likely be in my music playlist. I unironically *enjoy* Dad Rock, and anything synth-pop, or whatever the 80's would call avantgarde. Still, I graciously chose to accept this generous invitation from a guy in the work exchange team. It was an in attempt to have a personal experience with this widespread commotion.

But I must begin with an honest preface: I only struck up the valor to attend a music festival of this magnitude out of the fear of being left out. If it weren't for the sense of dissociation that I've felt with adults my own age, I would never willingly agree to sweat to overlong, lengthy wobble music. Choosing to attend this cultural party was a repeated attempt to try a slice of cake I desperately tried not to hate. *What if I have kids?* I thought. My future children will ask me what music festivals were like "back in my day", to which I otherwise wouldn't be able to respond to, if it weren't for this opportunity. My hypothetical offspring would deem me joyless and boring like I once did with my own parents. I felt like if I hadn't taken up this offer, there could be a possibility in the future that I might feel guilty for not being able to be a part of some kind of history.

So, it was into the wilderness I went.

As expected, preparation for an event like this was just as difficult as I thought it would be. Every article of clothing was chosen with careful apprehension and then later tossed away. I started over and over until my bed was covered by a mound of clothes. I studied the Google images of celebrities at Coachella like Vanessa Hudgens and the Jenner sisters. My basic understanding of festival fashion boiled down to a weird hybrid of bohemian-tribal-space- stripper. I decided against wearing a flower crown, fearful that I might blend in with everyone else. What could be worse than becoming a mere droplet in a sea of flower-crown-wearing sororities? Wearing a Native American headdress is undoubtedly wrong, but not as wrong as hundreds of girls disagreeing with that belief. I finally opted to choose comfort over style; a black halter top, a pair of jean shorts from last summer, and—with a prediction that I might have to walk for endless miles— an old pair of Chuck Taylors. Boring as it may be, I decided that the night would be for the real PLUR kittens. Let them shine, I say, for I am but an inconspicuous onlooker.

When I finally redeemed my tickets after a grueling three-hour wait in line, I noticed that, as far as my eyes could see, there were people whose ages ranged from late teens to mid-thirties in tawdry, showy attire. Girls wore neon fur boots in September and grown men wore latex animal heads. It raised my concern over their ability to be comfortable or even breathe, especially in the muggy Georgian heat. I presumed this level of "peacocking" could just be the unique act of courting one another. Or perhaps even one's way of setting free outside of normality, even if only for the next 48-hours. I quickly learnt that this was one of the only times in life where wearing jeans and sneakers would make anyone look out of place. I certainly came underdressed, just as I anticipated, which is an absurd thing to come to terms with since there were women who were only clothed in bedazzled bras and metallic bloomers.

"Oh, your outfit is stunning." I told a sweaty mermaid. Her face gleamed at my warm sentiment.

"Thank you soooo much!" she said, showing off pearly white teeth.

I was immediately gratified at how nice everyone was, especially the women. Ten years ago, in high school, it was automatically assumed that anything out of the ordinary would be mocked and humiliated. It had to be. It was somehow universally understood that the more intimidating you appeared to be to other girls, the more power you obtained. One time, in gym class, a popular girl with chemically damaged hair pointed out a quiet girl's frail, pale legs. We all began to call her "Bambi". There was absolutely nothing that this shy, Studio Ghibli enthusiast ever did to warrant such behavior from us. But this was the time when Paris Hilton was (most) girl's favorite archetype. It was also around the time the 2004 film *Mean Girls* came out: a film that slightly glamorized how animalistic and ruthless young girls can be, despite it being the complete opposite of what Tina Fey probably wanted to convey. The older I get, the more I realize that this generation of insecure teenagers I belonged to thankfully outgrew this toxic mentality and grew to be accepting and kind.

My mermaid friend then proceeded to take a strong hit off a chubby joint and extended an offer to me. If there's anything I've learned from EDM culture, it's that if you don't bring your own drugs, other people will supplement them for you. It's an act of hospitality. It's like visiting your grandma, but instead of being offered those dry ass pecan shortbread cookies or cherry cordials, it's Schedule II narcotics. I took a pull from a joint that was stained with metallic green lipstick. I was now best friends with a myriad of glittery, mythological aquatic/space creatures. They knew that this was my first time at a festival, and they expressed their endearment by touching their chest and cooing *awww* like I was a tween who had just started her first period.

"Let us know if you need anything. Water, food, acid, or just, you know, some people to talk to."

I thanked her for her goodwill and bid farewell to my new friends as they scampered into the horizon.

By this time, the day was a few minutes shy of seeing sunset, but the 840-acre structure was now illuminated by glow-in-the-dark hoola hoops and LED gloves to, I guess, visually stimulate or heighten one's psychedelic effects. The set designs were mammoth and bright, irradiating the faces of the crowd with purple and green. The main purpose of this was is to amplify the energy of the DJ. This evokes curiosity: Is there an alternate festival for people with photosensitive health concerns like epilepsy? Where do these people go? Would their experiences at EDM concerts be just as glitzy without the art installations, or would it be underwhelming in contrast? Exactly how crucial is visual aid for this music genre? In Fleetwood Mac's 1977's *Rumours* Tour, concertgoers were much too entranced by Stevie Nick's undeniable, entrancing aura to care about anything else, and all she ever did was sway-dance with a shawl. Marilyn Manson ripped up pages from a bible during one of his tours. But these are both musicians that are blessed with a special kind of charm and charisma; DJ's don't have to be. Things like charm and charisma are not necessarily needed to be a good DJ, which is why I was staring at disorienting images through a 100-foot LED screen and not them. We don't want to stare at men twisting knobs all night. We need the visual stimulation.

In this aspect of EDM culture, it is assumed that drugs play an important part. I know this because a white guy next to me was shaking and rocking back and forth into a drug-induced psychosis. His eyes darted left and right, teeth grinded together, as his friends surrounded him with water bottles. One friend attempted to comfort him with affirmations like, "It's all in your head, dude!" and "Just chill out!". Moments later, a medic team came by and shined a light into his eyes. They asked him how much ecstasy he took.

"He took, like, maybe a point and a half." his friend interjected.

They pulled him up from off the ground and onto his feet, and now walked with the team of medics who all acted as though this was normalcy. Everybody seemed to act like this was normalcy. And this is precisely where a huge part of my alienation from these people came from: my own personal inability to do drugs. Now, this is not to say that I have not *accepted* to do drugs in the past. There were many times in my early twenties when I reflexively always said yes to drugs despite knowing that I had a history of having soul-crushing, horrifying experiences. During one of the South's worst winter storms, 2013's Snowpocalypse as we Atlantans call it, (so two inches of snow on the roads and a scarcity of bread and milk) some friends and I were stuck at a shroom dealer's house. We had nothing to do and no alcohol, so he offered us free shrooms. I said yes. I ate this hallucinogen which tasted like dirty gym socks. When I told him that I regretted this decision, he looked at me with a menacing smile and said, "It's too late to turn back now!"; this is probably one of the top five things you *don't* tell a person who is about to peak on drugs. Within forty-five minutes, I felt like I was ascending into the afterlife, fully convinced that I was going to die. My friend stroked my hair and told me that I was fine, but I felt like she was lying. I felt like she tried to keep my inevitable death a secret from me and she wanted me to die peacefully along with the delusional hope that I was going to make it through the night. More and more people came in and out of the room, people I didn't know, whose joyful faces turned sinister and evil. His girlfriend turned off the lights and played "Humming" by Portishead on the record player. It's a song that makes you feels like you are being abducted by extraterrestrials due to lead singer Beth Gibbons' vibrato, as well as the song's usage of the theremin, an instrument invented in the 20's that emits a ghostly, ethereal sound. It triggered a seven-hour panic attack. My friends had to convince me that I wasn't actually dying.

This doom in my chest lasted for 6 hours.

Another time, an ex-boyfriend named Alex and I chose to stay in on Valentine's Day one year and opted to do acid instead. We took two hits each and waited. On his bed, we laid on our backs, talked about something work-related and then suddenly the popcorn ceiling began to move. Then the framed paintings of waterfalls began to move as if the water was actually flowing. He grabbed the headboard and clenched his jaw, I watched as every hair on his beard appeared to be dancing. Once we were on the peak of that rollercoaster, we watched David Bowie music videos which then, for some reason, inspired me to cry about the abortion we had. I never did psychedelics after that.

* * *

There was still so much to uncover and digest for a festie-virgin such as myself, but I was more ravenous for carnival food than drum and bass. Through the thick smog of sage and marijuana, the sweet aroma of corndogs and churros lured me in. I waited in line for a $13 turkey leg as a short, stocky redheaded man in black clothes approached me in a golf cart.

"How ya doin'?" he asked in a slow, southern drawl.

"Hungry." I shrugged with my arms crossed.

"Are you enjoying the festival so far? Borgore is about to come on."

"Oh, well I—"

"—Yeah, this looks a lot bigger than last year. We're

seeing a huge growth with this festival."

"I've never actually been before. This is my first festival...ever." I explained.

His eyes widened like I had just told him a sacrilegious secret.

"Oh, you're kidding!" He exclaimed. "Well, would you like a tour?"

As tantalizing as the idea of turkey legs were at the time, I swiftly decided to skip the winding line of deep-fried food and hop on the back of this stranger's golf cart.

"Hold on tight, now."

We accelerated with the loud mechanical whirring, now careening through crowds as he stopped, greeted friends, and intermittently took sips from his red solo cup. He took me backstage where an artist named Rusko was playing a set, a blonde male with a trendy haircut who looked like every guy I've ever met at a suburban house party who sold cocaine. My courteous new friend hopped off his low-speed vehicle and extended a hand like a true southern gentleman as he ushered me onto safe ground.

"Follow me," he said. And that is exactly what I did. We navigated through security and climbed on stage. Into the horizon, a beautiful constellation of different people of different age, creed, and race danced like a moving swarm. The stage lights flickered different colors. The smoke machines spewed, and the pyrotechnics blasted periodically in the right moments. The energy was palpable. Electricity was in the air. Nobody said a word, but there was no need for words when a universal emotion was being felt. Despite how you might feel about the culture and the ludicrous, sometimes dangerous aspects that it often entails, there is no denying that the whole belief system of "Peace, Love, Unity and Respect" is society's solid attempt to heal and escape. I thanked the red-headed stranger for this memorable opportunity and hugged him. With an hour drive ahead of me and the mental and physical exhaustion of walking in the heat for nine hours, it was time to head home. I unwrapped the Day-2 Passes from around my wrist and handed it to a white guy with dreadlocks on my way out.

Although my initial intention was to do research, I surprised myself by being able to say that I interacted with a crowd of thousands and danced along to the squelching dubstep sounds. What I've learned is this: in a generation where mass shootings run rampant, our enemies are in power, our idols are dropping dead one suicide at a time, and technology has made us less connected, one thing is for sure: the importance of music festivals lies within the magic of unity. The women are beautiful. The music is loud. The art is abundant. No matter who you are or where you come from, acceptance and respect are two virtues that are obvious in the atmosphere. It is, by and large, what we wish reality could always be.

NAKED ON THE INTERNET

One of the weirdest things about your mid-twenties, is having to ask yourself a very important question: what is the appropriate time to tell someone you've just met about the impending doom you feel in your chest? What about childhood trauma? It would be easier for me to find a one-night stand to distract myself from the big questions, but instead, I navigate through an overwhelmingly large crowd with a forced look of contentment.

I don't know why I'm at this party. It started with waking up with the paralyzing fear that I have not left my house in weeks and that my friends might have moved on without me. I agreed to attend this party but mainly out of guilt, fear, and the promise of an open bar. There are days when the simple presence of another human being feels like warm linen sheets in the springtime because it makes me feel like everything will be alright. There even comes a point when I feel like it's absolutely necessary for me to be around friends, because listening to other people's problems takes my mind off of my own. It's a sweet relief from myself. It's the idea that the internal conflicts in my life are nothing more and nothing less than human normality. *I dropped out of college for the second time this summer, but you contracted herpes. We are one. We're going to be okay, you and me.*

Other days, it sounds like the worst thing. I will wake up some days and the idea of small talk makes me want to rip out hangnails with my teeth. The phone will ring and I will watch as it turns into a missed call and it's almost as if I can feel the disappointment growing on their faces. You feel guilty for selfishly putting your own comfort in front of their needs as a friend, but you'll always let it surpass. I mean, it'll be five o' clock on a Wednesday afternoon and you haven't even brushed your teeth yet. You'll still be wearing the oversized t-shirt from the night before because you have no energy to practice basic self-care. And if that's the case, you won't have enough energy to entertain anyone either.

This is one of those days.

I hardly know any of these people aside from faces I am only familiar with as their identities on Instagram, and my friends who are too busy hosting guests. I am an abandoned puppy in a cardboard box and everyone can sense my suffering. I begin to fear that people will only begin to start conversations with me out of pity and the room is suddenly smaller and humid like the inside of the shoe. I'm panicking. I move through the crowd, prying my body from every angle of sweaty strangers, and make my way to the restroom. I have no need to use it, but a few moments of isolation seem like a safe refuge from socializing. The lights flicker on. I sit on the toilet seat cover and pull out my phone. There are many things a person suffering from social anxiety might be afraid of (death, heartbreak, existence, disappointment, confusion, the insatiable void within yourself, etc.) but the most terrifying of all is a phone with low battery. I have only a moment before my screen turns black, but I sacrifice it for a few minutes of Facebook, Twitter, Instagram, Tumblr, Gmail, Pinterest, and YouTube. I feel the stillness of peace. I feel infinite. And then screen goes black.

The internet provides a sense of control that I lack in real life; I can remove someone from my world or choose who I allow in. I can remove myself from the ability of existing to them, and most importantly, I can control how I exist to those I choose to exist *to*.

And that is important to me.

In real life, I can't fuck with physics, therefore I cannot magically appear whenever somebody is talking about me. I have no control over how I might exist to them and I cannot keep people from having a concept of me in their head. *Object permanence*, the understanding that something still exists even though it may not be observed in front of you, is fucking terrifying. But in a pixelated utopia such as the internet, I don't have to worry about quinoa stuck in my teeth, therefore I choose to showcase the best possible version of myself. I can emulate the best parts of myself and embody that just by withholding the darker, sadder parts. Sometimes when I feel anxious and confused about my sense of self, I like to change my entire identity by way of a new username and a new profile picture. I find it comforting that it's always a lot easier to start over existentially on the internet. It's not so readily believable in real life.

The World Wide Web is also where you can ask the big questions. You can safely come forth with your suffering. Conversely, in real life, you can't say, "I starve to punish myself from time to time" on a first date. You have to sell yourself and cram your craziness behind a door until you can fool someone into loving you unconditionally enough to accept what's actually behind it.

On Twitter, there is something easier about neurotically spilling the details of your personal issues to complete strangers in 140 characters or less. The same wouldn't be as easy to do with, say, my mother. I don't need her to know that the lack of intimacy and physical affection from my childhood has affected my sex life in my adulthood, but a teenager from Topeka, Kansas will understand the correlation between fellatio and my inner torment. We relate, somehow. The pain is useful here.

I haven't completely figured out exactly why I feel more connected to strangers than I ever have with people in reality. My theory is that the people I know in real life are unapologetic and merciless in the way they judge me. One summer, a photographer asked me to be a part of a body paint series.

"The only thing is that you will be completely nude. Are you comfortable with that?" he asked.

I felt a slight tremble in my voice in the same way a

nervous Kindergartner would, but as the word *yes* spilled out, there was no denying that within that moment I felt *good*. The agreement felt seamless and organic; I made an important decision for myself without having to seek approval from a boyfriend or a family. I didn't know it yet, but I was taking back total control over a body that never felt truly mine. It wasn't until I was naked in the woods, covered in black paint, that I felt beautiful again. My social media brewed a series of mixed reactions; the negative reactions came from concerned family members who asked why I was "doing soft porn". It came from coworkers who asked why I needed the attention. It came from my boyfriend's group of close friends who wondered how he could be "so chill" about me exposing a body that was believed to be meant for him only. I had a friend tell me that she had to block me on all forms of social media because I was not a "positive" person. I was not *Chicken Noodle for the Soul* enough for her. I was not *Live Laugh Love* enough for her. I was not pure enough. And it fucked with me.

The positive reactions, however, came from girls I'd never met before, who admired me for being so vulnerable. They asked me what it took to be so fearless. I spent some time trying to process the praise as anything real or valid because I spent a long time believing the ones who criticized me for the same act instead. And that's the thing about a woman being naked, not only on the internet, but in general: to some, being naked on the internet is throwing yourselves into the wolves. It's brave. For others, it's decreasing your value. It's impure. What it means to be naked is subjective, and it varies in truth depending on who you ask. But why, exactly, do I receive an abundance of love and acceptance from strangers and not the ones who observe me in the flesh on a daily basis? In a room full of these people, real people with warm bodies and beating hearts, I am still consumed by crippling loneliness. I watch what I say, careful with tonality, cautious not to offend anyone in the room unless I want to apologize or explain myself later. But on the internet, I can tweet about dick and not think twice. The internet is a safe haven. It's a legendarium where I am God and I can control my very own world.

I have been in this bathroom for 20 minutes, but people are probably not looking for me. A person with social anxiety is good at one thing and one thing only: escape routes. The trick is to leave and do so gracefully without making a scene. Saying goodbye is the polite thing to do but will only result in everyone keeping you from what's important: leftover nachos and a warm bed. They will guilt you into staying and you'll only sit awkwardly chewing your cuticles until you think enough time has passed to try again, in which case you will sneak through the back door, or say you left something in your car. That's the frustrating thing about loving someone who struggles with both loving loneliness and hating loneliness; you have to be understanding as they decide which is true for them that day.

For some people, it's not a matter of when or where to ask the big questions, but to *who* we're asking the big questions to. I've been trying to seek acceptance and understanding from those in my life who couldn't readily give it to me. I'll always be more willing to overshare on the internet because health insurance doesn't totally cover therapy and counseling. Maybe a sense of anonymity has helped me find my people. Maybe the internet has allowed me to transform as whoever I want to be, as many times as I need. It's more believable to love a person when you are only able to see their edited version. Reality just isn't as forgiving.

SHARP TEETH

Psychopaths don't have sharp teeth. They won't tell you about their drinking problem or their personality disorder on the first date, and they most likely won't hit you on the second. They certainly won't be transparent about how they were neglected as a child or that their father's hostility manifested into self-hatred in their adulthood. Nobody would willingly ever choose to love an abuser, but that's what makes them so special; their irresistible charm and the charismatic way they exude a mysterious element of danger. Ray was someone who inhibited this extraordinary personality trait.

He had a hearty, infectious laugh and ways of making everybody feel loved and understood. I met him when I was 19. He was 24. At the time, he had no fixed address and was couch surfing at his friend's house. He owned one pair of red Chucks that he never wore socks with, a pair of jeans and two t-shirts. One was a white Fruit of the Loom undershirt with a hole in one of the armpits. The other one was a black t-shirt that was two sizes too small, with both of the sleeves cut off. Across the chest was a logo of a thrash-metal band in an illegible, spiky font. He had nothing besides these few things and a voracious need to destroy. Much to his benefit, I, on the other hand was young, impressionable, and curious. I lived my life within the confines of safety that my parents spent my entire life administering. Despite this, I saw just how much more thrilling life could be if I spent it with someone as dangerous and stimulating as Ray. The promise of adventure that he gave me in the beginning prompted me to follow in his footsteps. I became much like his very own ingénue. Before I could legally drink, he taught me his method of taking shots of liquor, the proper way: "Alright, coat your mouth with Coca-Cola first," he began. "Now take a swig of Jack but try not to smell it. Hold your breath, don't breathe."

I pour the whiskey in my mouth and swallowed while still holding my breath. "Atta girl, now chase it quickly with the soda again. See? Not so bad. Just do it over and over until you you're hammered."

The night we fell in love, we kissed in a room full of music equipment, beer cans, and a mattress on the floor. The room had Sharpie graffiti on the walls and someone even scribbled on the ceiling, *All It Takes Is Some Balls* which had absolutely no context, but it seemed to serve as a positive affirmation for anyone who needed to see it. As the room spun, I tried to maintain equilibrium while I laid on my back, staring at the inexplicable slogan. I wondered how many nights Ray must have done the same.

When we kissed for the first time, it reminded me of that exhilarating scene in the 1997 psychological thriller *Fear*. The one where emotionally disturbed bad boy Mark Wahlberg fingers the virginal teen queen Reese Witherspoon on a roller coaster until orgasm—all while "Wild Horses" by The Rolling Stones plays softly in the background. I still think about that a lot. It was a lot like that.

The first time we argued, he had suspicion that I was texting another man. I refused to hand over my phone, so he threw me out onto the front lawn and pushed my head into the dirt. I would presume that, to a normal person, a circumstance like this would inspire anyone to leave and never look back. When I found myself back in his bed the next day, I stopped trying to find logic in anything. Similar things have happened a few more times for different reasons, but we learned to slap bandages over the traumas and we never spoke of them again. He tried to overcompensate a few times with gifts and remorse, which was a cunning way to validate my optimism during the stagnant times. It worked for a while until his emotional instability—too large to hide under the bed at this point— was now sprawled across on display for everyone to see. His drinking became constant. What once was a social activity to bond with friends, became dissociation in his dark bedroom and slowly, he was bursting at the seams. At the right moment, a predator will strike with venom, and by the time the prey notices, they're already paralyzed and as good as dead. I knew—and he knew— that he could do anything to me and I would stay. This was precisely the reason why he didn't care to manage his anger anymore. He knew that he didn't *need* to change because I would have still stayed anyway. Simple things like playing videogames were too provoking. He once played Madden NFL 25 for seven consecutive hours, and when he lost a match, he propelled the controller at my flat screen TV. It left a crack that spread across the screen in abstract shapes and glitched colors. When he realized this meant he didn't have a TV to play video games on anymore, he got even more irritated. He then split the TV in half by throwing it onto the driveway. It was an excellent TV, given to me as a housewarming gift from my parents. At some point, I lied and told them that our apartment got broken into, and that these non-existent burglars must have destroyed it. When they asked about the broken table, I lied and said it must have also been destroyed during another home invasion although, in reality, Ray broke that too. Our home became collateral damage and there were craters in the drywall, scathed knuckles, and broken dishes.

I was great at lying to protect him. He once misplaced his paycheck and accused me of stealing it and he looked into my eyes for a moment with a blank stare that was soulless and cold, and punched me in the mouth. He hit me so hard that my canine punctured through my top lip and I looked down at my jeans and saw blood droplets making patterns onto my lap. I looked into my mirror and lost complete motor control; I didn't know how to process what just happened. Instead, I let out a yowling cry and whimpered powerlessly. He drove me to the Emergency

Room where I lied and told the nurses and doctors that I tripped down the stairs while running in a Snuggie. Nobody questioned it. My coworkers thought it was a hilarious story, calling me *Snuggie* at every opportunity: *Okay, Snuggie, there's a mandatory meeting on Monday. Don't be late.* My friends never asked about my stitches, and my parents only told me to be more careful next time. Lying to protect an abuser was both intuitive and shameful. In order to not be engulfed in the flames, I had to pull myself out of trance-inducing dissociation whenever my mind would focus on the humiliation. With four stitches holding my top lip together, I would sit at every mandatory staff meeting and fight every internal monologue that wanted to persuade me that I was, in fact, stupid and weak. Ray was a baby bird that I hid in my clasped hands.

One night during a Halloween party, a greasy guy dressed as Popeye the Sailor Man showed everyone his new tattoo. It was an Irish flag on his right bicep, and I touched it to see if it was real. A few moments later, everyone cleared the room to migrate outside for a cigarette break. Alone in the kitchen, I poured myself another shot of vodka until I felt a burly force on my shoulder. I was suddenly pinned against the refrigerator, the back of my head slammed against a blocky gift shop magnet from Universal Studios. Ray—who had bitten his lip so hard that it left bloody indents—inhaled and exhaled uncontrollably. He growled, "Did you just fucking touch him?" with my thick black hair tightly wrapped around his heavy hands. "We're leaving!" he'd order, as his fingertips dug into the meat of my arm as we made our way to the front door. I remember the terror and desperation I felt about being alone in a car with him, with nobody there to protect me. It was strange, the way he could disguise his inebriation and say goodbye to his friends so cheerfully to the point where no one would ever suspect a thing. Still, even as my face held an obvious look of *Oh god, please fucking help me,* no one blinked twice. The moment we made it around the corner, away from the house party, he began to swerve the car.

"You're such a stupid bitch." he muttered through clenched teeth.

We drove down a dark back road, weaving in and out of double yellow lines and he asked me if I was "ready to die today." I knew that at any moment, an 18-wheeler could careen the opposite direction and hit us head on, sending me through the windshield and Ray with a mouthful of broken glass. Under his fingertips, he navigated the steering wheel—in complete control of our lives— without looking at the road. I begged him to pull over, but he was unable to hear me above the noise of his own screaming and other cars honking.

Somehow, we made it home.

He took apart my phone and threw the pieces into the woods so that I couldn't call for help. When I tried to run out the front door, I felt clammy hands wrapped around my neck. The restricted airflow and lack of oxygen to the brain caused me to see stars. A second longer, I would have lost consciousness. When he woke up in the late afternoon the next day, he didn't remember anything. He drank so much vodka the night before that he had absolutely no recollection of what happened. I was still petrified—my back damp from cold sweat, as I sat and watched in disbelief while he scooped the marshmallow pieces in his bowl of cereal, as if nothing ever happened. If I would have died, he would have seen my lifeless body on the beige carpet and wouldn't know anything about it. Only until then, did I fully grasp the reality that being in a relationship with someone who was unable to manage their emotions (until violent psychosis) was what will bring me to my untimely death. *That's it*, I thought. *That's how I'm going to die.*

What is most interesting to me was how suspicion grew amongst our friends, yet nobody ever felt the need to ask if I was okay. On the one hand, who was going to stand up to this brawny mastodon? And most importantly, if anyone ever *did* decide to protect me, I most likely wouldn't let them. What nobody tells you about victims of domestic abuse is that we don't want to be saved. We want to see this whole thing through. Save us, offer us protection and a safe place, and we'll see it as intrusion: *Mind your business. I know what I'm doing. Stay out of my relationship. I know him better than you do. He's going to change. Thank you for your concern but I've got it under control.* In addition to this, most people have a hard time understanding *why* victims don't leave sooner. This will be the hardest, most complicated thing to try and explain to friends, family, and new boyfriends in the future. I was a naïve, impressionable teenager being controlled by an older abuser, who was skilled at keeping victims close.

When I explain this to someone, it's difficult to maintain cool-headed and not argumentative when they begin to question why I *stayed*, and not why he *abused* in the first place. It's strange how blaming the victim first is a knee-jerk reaction to any abuse story. Sure, it's easy to get confused as to why a woman would willingly stay in such a relationship. It's as if the answer is almost too simple to comprehend: I was a young girl with no self-esteem, looking for anything that could love me back. Ray was older, bigger, stronger, and had more of a responsibility, as a man, to not hit girls half his size and use them as rehabilitation centers. It was his own job to sort out his childhood traumas and manage his mental illness.

Besides, leaving was not a simple solution. Leaving was a process. It's worth mentioning that the abuse was never constant, so there was room for optimism to grow during the better times. The peaceful moments in between validated the small hope I had, and so I stayed a little longer. Even if I plotted an exit plan, I'd have only one opportunity to execute it. If I fail, then what? A trip to the emergency room? Death? It felt safer to stay, bite my tongue, and smile through the abuse. Until, of course, years went by and it was obvious that things were never going to get better. I realized that I was living in a nightmarish purgatory. The idea of leaving was still scary, but now, my determination outweighed that fear.

One day, his father called to invite us over for lunch. I agreed to go, but only if I could drive. When I pulled into the driveway of his dad's house, I kept the car running and pretended that I had a missed call from my mom.

"Go ahead and go inside without me. I'll be right behind you. I have to return this call." I insisted. Hesitating, he demanded: "Alright, hurry up." I watched him enter inside the house. As soon as he closed the door behind him, I put the car in reverse and drove away. That was it. That was literally fucking it. I turned my phone off because I knew he'd eventually realize I was gone and would try to call my phone to con me into changing my mind. I'd look in the rearview mirror, frantically, to make sure he didn't steal his dad's car to chase me down. *What did I just do?* I'd think to myself. *I didn't think I'd make it this far.* I was so concentrated on orchestrating the actual exit plan that I overlooked the second half of the strategy: *Where do I go now?* In a panic, I drove to a friend's house that was only a few miles away. Looking over my shoulder like a paranoid schizophrenic, I knocked on her door, but it was her dad who answered. He looked surprised to see me. "Come on in" he said, immediately recognizing that something was wrong. On the sofa in the living room, I told him the entire history of the abuse. Against my will, he took me to the police station. A police officer with a short crew cut and blue-mirrored sunglasses on the top of his head told me, "I've been doing this for 30 years. You would have either died or went to jail if you stayed." I was told I did the right thing, yet, strangely, I didn't feel any kind of victory immediately. I was actually overcome with grief over the loss of a best friend. I felt tremendous guilt for abandoning someone who needed me. I felt stupid for feeling it, as anyone with a brain would, but I was helpless.

After all, Ray really wasn't a monster in totality; the

violence and the anger were just louder than the less aggressive personality traits. It would have been easier to leave someone who inhabited *only* those negative characteristics, but for the longest time, I felt like my favorite parts of him could balance out the bad. Sure, there were times when loving him felt as though I was Shelley Duvall's character in *The Shining*, swatting a manic Jack Nicholson away with a bat, fighting for my life and living a hellish nightmare. But it wasn't always like that. In particular, I loved how protected and safe I was from the world with him nearby. I could walk around at any party, do what I want, talk however I wanted, and didn't have to worry about who would react. I had a 6'1, 260-pound football quarterback for a boyfriend who was always ready to break jaws. At times, it even seemed as though he was looking for somebody's face to use as an outlet for his anguish. No one dared to touch or cross me. Unfortunately, and ironically, Ray wasn't able to protect me from himself. When he was happy, though, life was fun. He once drove me out to go on a whimsical adventure. We walked through miles of knee-high grass until we reached a point where he covered my eyes with his hands and told me he had a surprise waiting at the end of our walk. When he unveiled me, we were at the top of a mountain, overlooking a rock quarry where *The Walking Dead* was filmed. It was only us and acres of natural beauty. We drank beer and swam in the turquoise lagoon until nightfall, almost getting lost.

Since then, I knew I could rely on him to provide this kind of hedonistic fun on a consistent basis. Life was more colorful and had a certain kind of vitality that I didn't have before meeting him. I'll always remember the violence, just as much as I'll always remember the summer when we trespassed and got leeches while swimming in unknown waters. I'll remember the nights spent at bars, looking the best I ever did, stalling time and enjoying my youth, and all the friendships I made from being Ray's girlfriend. "Don't ever let anyone in this world make you feel like you don't matter. Write." he once said to me. For a moment, his eyes had tenderness and—for once—they didn't seem reptilian and unpredictable. I loved him the way Jacqueline Kennedy Onassis felt about John F. Kennedy in her letters:

Mrs. Jacqueline Kennedy
November 22, 1963

And I remember when I met him, it was so clear that he was the only one for me. We both knew it, right away. And as the years went on, things got more difficult—we were faced with more challenges. I begged him to stay. Try to remember what we had at the beginning. He was charismatic, magnetic, and electric and everybody knew it. When he walked, every woman's head turned, everybody stood up to talk to him. He was like this hybrid, this mix of a man who couldn't contain himself. I always got the sense that he became torn between being a good person and missing out on all of the opportunities that life could offer a man as magnetic as him. And in that way, I understood and loved him. I loved him, I loved him, I loved him. And I still love him. I love him.

When my mind begins to romanticize him, I try to focus on my freedom from the darkness. I train my mind to appreciate it instead. I still have nightmares where I find myself back with him, and the terror of figuring out how to escape engulfs me the same way the dread once did. I wake up and must remind myself that I'm safe. I now have a body that he will never touch again. I'd spend the next few years and maybe even the rest of my life trying to unlearn what love is. Love was painful and violent. Love was passion, but not the good kind. I wasted the better half of my twenties to abuse but choosing to take back my life after being given a second chance meant that I no longer had to live it in fear. I couldn't let his abuse cheat me out of something good. I am worth more than what I was given in the past. I knew that, someday, I'll eventually find someone who will not only know how to *take* the love that I have to give but can *give* and reciprocate it back. Redefining love, what it once looked like and what it means to me now, will be the hardest part. But I did love him. I loved him, I loved him.

LUST, ACTUALLY

What's more exhilarating than lying naked in bed with a man who doesn't love you? A few times in life do we come across people who can never give us the love that we want but are still somehow able to convince us that their lust is more fulfilling. My favorite thing to do when coming across these people, is to project my expectations and hopes onto them. I especially find it more engaging if they are emotionally incapable of honoring them, and even more if they can exist to me as something I can be addicted to. I was infatuated with one particular man who was both. He provided my life with excitement and magic, even if it was brief and unrequited.

He stood tall and beautiful like a marble statue, distinctly brawny and too prominent to overlook in a room, an urban lumberjack. He had an auburn beard that contrasted his Irish skin and a steely blue gaze that peered in fixation. He was an established, young professional working in a city he pretended to hate. I met him at a single's mixer in an affluent uptown lounge that serves as a watering hole for expensive escorts, rich men, and college students. He politely introduced himself with two Knob Creek on the rocks as a friendly proposal. I accepted this offering, naturally, as he adjusted his plaid bowtie and extended a large hand.

"Hey, how are you?" he began, coolly. "I'm the host of this event tonight."
We clinked our glass tumblers and said cheers, maintaining full eye contact as we knocked the bourbon down our throats. He answered three and a half questions before he reached into the inner pocket of his tweed tuxedo jacket and pulled out a business card.

"Here's my name," he said. "Look me up on Facebook. I should be the first one that shows up."
Looking retrospectively at this, it was a maniacally narcissistic thing to say. He politely excused himself and returned to mingle with the crowd. I lost him to a swarm of socialites and bottle service girls.

Later that night, I laid in bed and pondered over my strange encounter with this enigmatic weirdo. This prompted me to scour the deep pockets of my coat for his business card. Egg shell finish. Off-white coloring. Tasteful thickness. I brushed my finger along the black lettering of his name. I typed in his first name in a search bar and, as he promised, found his profile before I even got to the first letter of his last name. Add friend.

Shortly after, I receive a message:
It was nice to meet you.
"Thanks for the drink!" I typed back.
Three animated dots appeared, and then nothing.

Seven minutes later, a metallic ding:

"I remember you mentioning to me that you're a writer. I'm hosting a party at my house this weekend. If you'd like, you're more than welcome to stop by. I'd love to hear about your creative goals and offer any help where I can."

Normally, this would be the point where I disengage. The last place I would expect to find love would be in a VIP section on a Wednesday night. The nightlife belonged to eligible bachelors, all who are mostly married men with expendable income and fraternity brothers with Chlamydia. As a general rule, I know better than to give out my number.

"Sounds good. Here's my number." I replied.
If he was a sleazy creep, it was worth discovering for myself.

When I arrived at his front-step that Saturday night, he answered the door wearing nothing but a blue velvet robe, a yacht cap, and a tobacco pipe hanging on his lips.

"Come on in," he said. "There's beer in the fridge, grab whatever you'd like." He had Coltrane playing on vinyl and his house was decorated with kitschy relics of Americana and vintage film posters. There were beautiful people everywhere; red-lipped brunettes sitting cross-legged on the couch, blondes with high-cheekbones and trendy haircuts, and bearded guys drinking local IPA's, doodled with Sailor Jerry-style tattoos. The environment, both buzzing and visually stimulating, forced participants to mingle and network. I faintly recall conversing about feminism with a girl who had pointy eyebrows and jet-black hair. She explained—in a long, drawn-out, San

Fernando Valley accent—her disbelief in the movement and, on the contrary, how white men had it harder in society. I excused myself to the bathroom hoping she wouldn't be there when I returned.

As the night progressed, the house slowly cleared out. One by one, attendees retrieved their Ubers which was indicative to me it was time that I too should bid farewell. I swung my purse over my shoulder and headed for the front door just as *he* entered the room. He noticed I had my belongings.

"You outta here too?" he asked, almost pleadingly. "Stay awhile. I feel like we haven't seen each other all night."

He reached for a bottle of bourbon, poured two room temperature shots, and offered me the smaller one. I took off my coat. I knocked down the bourbon, trying to disguise the look of hot pain racing down my esophagus. On the coffee table, a black Polaroid 600 sat on top of a stack of vintage Playboy Magazines.

"Does this old thing work?" I asked, pointing.

He nodded and sat his glass down.

"Wanna take trashy pictures?" he asked.

"Yes."

We migrated to his backyard, where fuchsia azaleas and lush monkey grass grew rampant. He aimed the camera at me, moving it horizontally, vertically, and then horizontally again before capturing the moment.

"Smile." he ordered.

"I don't smile."

"But you have a pretty one."

My tongue brushes over my crooked teeth. I felt like he was lying. Still, his attention felt like hot honey pouring on top of my head. I felt an unfamiliar warmness throughout my entire body. He sensed how self-conscious I was. He wanted me to bloom, but I remained a tight bud.

"Here," he took his yacht captain hat off.

"Put this on."

He positioned the hat perfectly on my head and swept the stray hairs away. His knuckles grazed my skin, goosebumps spreading. The hat was three sizes too big and constantly slid off onto the bridge of my nose. I laughed out of nervousness and then a bright light flashed, followed by a loud camera shutter. I understood then why women felt comfortable around his presence. He had a way of making girls feel beautiful. He encouraged them to see themselves in the same light he saw them in.

As we made our way back inside the house, he handed me one of the polaroid photos and kept the other one for himself to add to the collection of beautiful women on his refrigerator. Like a child seeking praise for their amateur macaroni arts-and-crafts project, the collection of aspiring models and Suicide Girls magnetized onto his fridge seemed like a sanctum of some sort, a place of high honor. I sat on the kitchen counter next to the sink and toyed with the antique pistol that he kept in the back of a silverware drawer. I studied the weight and fingered the trigger, overwhelmed and in awe of its potential power. He talked about his belief in the Second Amendment rights and Morrissey. "His voice is just so dry and mechanical." he shrugged, unapologetic about his opinion. He dug into the icy depths of an Igloo cooler for a beer. He belonged to that elite tier of *cool guy* that I hated. He was so disapproving, unimpressed, and cynical of music and just about everything else. When I asked him an obscure question about pop culture, he replied with a quasi-philosophical quote by Tom Waits. As the night turned into early morning, he stretched his Herculean arms and yawned. "Well, I'm going to bed. It was very nice talking to you tonight, Jen. Let me know when you want to do this again." It was inarguably the politest way to end the night with someone. Yet, somehow, I was surprised and even impressed that he decided to end the night when most men would lure a woman into bed with them. I said goodnight and left.

For years after this, we grew closer as friends. As aspiring actresses and bottle service girls came in and out through the revolving door of his dating life, our friendship remained sincere because we kept it strictly platonic. I was okay with this mainly because I had witnessed the way he would charmingly drive women into madness. I felt, in a weird way, more fortunate than them. I knew that as long as our friendship was chaste and pure, there could be no room for bitterness to grow. I found it more satisfying that way, particularly when I saw his ex-girlfriend, a more ethnically ambiguous and heavily tattooed Alyssa Milano, sullenly sit on his front porch with her head in her hands after an argument. I remember grinning from ear-to-ear.

And then, one summer, he— by choice—decided to be single and abstained from dating indefinitely. It was then things started to become overtly sexual. He'd pull down my neckline and expose my terracotta nipples and I'd blush, giggle, and say *stop* but what I really meant to say was *fill all my existential holes and compensate for my lack of affection from my childhood.* I started to become addicted to his attention. It was strange for us both—me, especially. It never used to be something I thought I would ever want. Even when we would dress up for a night out, where I'd twirl and show off the bouncy, ruffle trim of my dress, we were always able to acknowledge each other's attractiveness, but only in the same way one would respectfully admire art from a distance. Now, however, this dynamic was changing.

On one of the hottest days of the summer, we walked around the city with the sweet perfume of July hanging in the air. We started a tab at the kind of gentrified, artisan sandwich bar that played Danzig on the jukebox and served Rosé slushies. He'd been drinking warm beer in my passenger seat on the way there and was in the state of drunkenness that I liked; it was the only time he'd ever allow himself to be vulnerable to anyone. Sober, he was like chamomile tea and milk; cloudy and opaque. It was never clear whether his mind was somewhere else or here with me. The less concise and transparent he was willing to be, the more his mystery compelled me, and the more I realized that he'd eventually become a knot I would have to spend days trying to untie. He began redirecting every topic back to stories about past relationships and there was this distinctive way he spoke about ex-girlfriends that antagonized me; disdainful in the beginning until it slowly turned into yearning, and then regret. I watched as he silently fought the battle between torment and apathy.

We ended up on the rooftop during the time of evening when the sun was slowly sinking into a vermillion horizon. My heels dug into the AstroTurf and the world began to tilt, the champagne made my eyes glossy and my chest a splotchy red. I loomed over the balcony, overlooking rush hour traffic in a malaise stupor, admiring the city neither he, nor I, would ever get out of. A warm, sweaty hand cupped my face and I sat up straight. I puckered my lips, opened my eyes, and realized instantly that he wasn't aiming for my mouth. There was a look of shock on his face.

He said, "I was... trying to kiss you on the forehead." The mortification felt like fire ants swarming my chest. What was most startling to me was how I was— instinctively and without thought—ready for it to happen. I walked away, picking at my skin. He grabbed my arm and pulled me close:
"Were you going to kiss me? You were going to kiss me!" he teased.

"I was not."
He leaned in and I met him halfway until our lips met. His face beamed, showing a toothy smile. We both pulled away, half-laughing and electrified at how we overstepped an important boundary.

What was it that I was feeling at that moment? There is something magical in the beginning of every romance. Everything is reborn again and life becomes more interesting. There's now a more important reason to practice self-care; shaving your legs, rubbing floral and fruity perfume onto your pulse points, motivation to look and feel your best. I am not enough to save me from myself. Only beautiful, tall men can. The magic lies in the mystery, the *not knowing*, of what is to come in even a week's time. I find potentiality more fun than the real thing. The real thing—love, maybe— is disappointing and painful. Every day, you must make the decision to love this person or not. Desire is the opposite; desire is finding temporary relief for your every emotional itch. To desire is to love without the emotional labor or responsibility and to follow your primal urges down the rabbit hole. That seemed to be perfect for him. And, with the electricity I felt in my fingertips, I decided that it was perfect for me too.

Since then, our texting became an exhilarating thing that felt like a direct hit of dopamine during random times of the day:

Him: *Kiss me again?*

Me: it's all i've been thinking about lol

Him: *When can I see you?*

Me: tuesday. i am coming over with burritos and beer.

Him: *Wear those heels that I like. The strappy ones that lace around your ankles.*

It brought a glowing beam to my face in public, noticeable enough for my friends to become inquisitive, but I had to honor our pact of secrecy. I would stealthily text underneath the table linen at a dinner with friends, turn off the sound when I was on dates with other boys. No matter where I was or who I was with, my head was either swimming in recent memories with him or the anticipation to make new ones.

When I showed up to his house that Tuesday, the door swung open and his eyes scanned me from head to toe before he greeted me with a wry smile. He grabbed the brown paper bag, heavy with steak burritos and tortilla chips, along with the 6-pack of Miller Lite tallboys, and set them down on the table before picking me up with one arm. He tossed me onto the springy mattress. He pushed my hair out of the way and touched my thighs as we moaned into each other's mouths. His hand melted onto my skin like velveteen. I rubbed his erection through the rough denim of his 501 Levi's. He pulled away, stood above me and unbuckled his belt. The initial pangs in my chest ensued; I could feel it in my throat. I undressed as he took off his clothes and tore the foil of the condom wrapper with his teeth. I thought to myself, *this is it, there is no turning back*, and it was as if my eyes communicated that thought, because his impish eyes had the same look. He entered me, I let out a gasp. We rolled around the light blue linen sheets on his bed as I dug my nails into his shoulder blades. He was bossy and domineering at first, like a hipster Christian Grey, throwing orders around for me to *switch positions, push my tits together, play with my clit*. And then came the tenderness, the soft kisses, until it ended with his large hand wrapped around my neck and cutting my air supply until I was on the edge of orgasm. There was a warmth in my pussy that went away, came back, and then got warmer. When the pressure became too great, my legs shook, and I was overcome with a wave of light-headedness until I surrendered to the twitching sensitivity of an orgasm. He let out a long, guttural *mmmh* before he came in the condom as I massaged his balls. We both rested on our backs, panting and catching our breath. Not a single word was exchanged, we were just buzzed by a feeling as if we had crossed a line that we could never uncross. We cleaned ourselves off with a towel and then silently put our clothes back on. He asked if I wanted any coffee to which I said yes. He went to the kitchen as I went to the bathroom to pee and reapply my lipstick.

We met in the living room where a steaming, Hawaiian-imported coffee was waiting for me on a table coaster. He turned on the Hallmark channel to a Christmas special starring Lacey Chabert, which, for some reason, inspired us to begin to talk about politics. It was amusing the way we acted like nothing happened. We sat together, repressing the fact that only moments ago his fingers were in my mouth. I enjoyed the fact that he could wrap my hair around his fist and fuck me one second and then talk about the political climate of our country the next. He went on to rant about foreign policy, but I focused more on how burly his arms looked in a heather gray cardigan and the way his unkempt hair was beginning to grow S-shaped curls.

Each time we were in each other's company after that, I noticed something weird happening: I was stubbing my toe on every bed frame corner, I stroked my hair until strands fell, and the thudding in my chest made it harder to enjoy casual conversations. As a teenager, I learned that this was the normal response to being around your crush but, nonetheless, I felt somewhat saddened by this. I felt like it was my fault for turning a normal friend into someone special, a plaything that elicited a dopamine response large enough for me to act like a fucking idiot. I knew that using him as a source of excitement could ultimately end as a bad decision. But for how long would he serve as a resource for this high? Every form of affection he'd show me felt like what '*O Magnum Mysterium*' sounds like.

Him: *Every time we kiss I want to tear off your clothes. Every time.*

His words became the sound of a choir's singing bouncing off the walls of a cathedral.

Him: *I can't stop thinking about your lips. Sorry.*

Mozart's Symphony No.40 in G minor.

He told me that he was going up north to the mountains to visit his dad and I felt like I was already coming down from the high, so I texted him really stupid things throughout the day just so I could live off of the little bit of attention he was willing to give.

Me: what's ur dad like?

Him: *Gene Hackman from the Royal Tenenbaums.*

Me: if i'm margot then who does that make you?

Him: *Wes Anderson.*

Any person would have been sickened by the banality of sexting between two quirky film buffs, but I felt as if it was true: if he was Wes Anderson, I was flattered to play a female role in his visually distinctive world. I was happy to be his muse for the time being, even if I could only play a cameo role.

We met frequently at a dive bar down the street, polishing off a bottle of scotch until crystalline glassware piled up around us. We'd stumble into a cab headed to his house in Cabbagetown. In public, he was distant; only rubbing my back as a means of affection whenever it felt safe to, or if our friends were too distracted. Sometimes, during last call, patrons of the dive bar would be too busy drunkenly swinging their hips to Elvin Bishop's *Fooled Around and Fell in Love* that nobody paid attention when he snuck in a kiss. He'd buy me cocktails and interject when drunk men tried to converse with me.

At home, he was attentive and talkative. He'd play Waylon Jennings, Merle Haggard, and other outlaw country music I'd never heard of. "Johnny Cash always got all the credit, but Waylon was the best outlaw," he'd argue. He'd lay his head on my lap while I raked his mahogany curls, his fingers laced together on his chest. His eyes were glossy, he was at that state of inebriation again.

"I like your perfume," he began.

"What is that? Vanilla? English rose? You smell like my ex-girlfriend."

"I'm not your ex-girlfrie—"

"—She *loved* roses and baby's breath. Every Tuesday I'd take her to the Farmer's Market and we'd eat Venezuelan arepas. Then, I'd pick up a bouquet for her just for it to die by the windowsill in her studio apartment."

I responded dryly, flatly, "Baby's breath?"

"A weird name for a flower, right? I looked it up on

Google and apparently it signifies everlasting love. Which is ironic," he scoffed.

"It's kind of cliché." I shrugged.

"So was she."

I'd lazily chuckle, pretending to go with his sense of humor although I knew it was a defense mechanism for his longing. "Yeah, roses and baby's breath," he said, mid-sip, knocking off the choreography of his consumption of Miller Lite in the bottle. "Those were her favorites."

* * *

Him: *You were amazing the other night.*

This was the text that I received in the middle of comparing different kombucha at Whole Foods. I didn't feel the dizzying affect that his text usually would. I felt morose over the fact that our friendship had come down to sex, only interested in seeing each other if orgasming could be involved.

Me: let's go have dinner plz. spend the day with me. we used to always have sunday fundays.

Him: *My schedule is pretty hectic this week.*

Me: every time i'm around u, it feels like a dozen golden retriever puppies. i feel like i am 2 greedy with ur time. why couldn't i have met u earlier in life?

Hours passed.

Him: *I need you to focus on yourself.*

I swallowed a hot lump in my throat.

Him: *Besides, I like what we have just as it is. I like the naiveté of it, the innocence. It's like we're teenagers again.*

We'd come to this discussion again later, face-to-face, at our favorite bar, only this time he was more blatant:

"I can't be your boyfriend. And you know that."

A waitress checked on us silently by putting her thumbs up. He raised his beer signifying her to bring another round. I combatted his honesty with my own:

"I wouldn't want you to be mine anyway. You'd make me miserable for six months and leave me for an actress."

He winked, shooting me with a make-believe gun with his thumb and index finger before walking away to the bathroom. I was left alone with the feeling of rejection and a half empty pint glass.

Why was I disappointed at the truth? Why did he even have to say it? I knew it already. His argument had merit. How could he ever be mine? He was just as much of a heartbroken fool as I was; jaded and running on empty from our past. I was just mostly upset at his method of delivery. He said it cleverly in a way that sounded like it was for *my* best interest but, in actuality, it was for his own. His unwillingness to love me felt more like an excuse, a card he kept in his wallet that he'd been saving to get out of this exact instance. It said, *See? I'm morally responsible enough to save you from more heartbreak* but it was really, *I don't have the emotional capacity to care for you in the way that you want.*

That night, there was no elation on his face, only a weird ambiguous smirk that came out of politeness whenever I tried to talk to him about anything. I'd sit on his couch watching cult classic films while he worked on his laptop, silently, if it weren't for the clicking sound of his fingertips on the keyboard. 45-minutes passed before he closed his laptop shut.

"Shall we go in my room?" he asked.

"Yeah."

He pulled my t-shirt over my head, threw it across the room, and laid me down. He kissed me but I felt nothing. It didn't make me feel woozy and disoriented like it did in the past. He lifted my skirt and fingered me until the butterflies in my stomach began to feel like a throbbing sensation. He slid his fingers in then out, stuck together by my slippery, soapy fluid. He laid on top of me, thrusting, as I let out small sighs and then came that long, guttural *mmmmh*. He kissed me on the forehead which he'd never done post-coitus before. He sat up at the end of the bed with a towel covering himself. I dressed myself and slid my shoes on.

"I'm going to head out."

A long pause.

"Okay, let me just get dressed and I'll walk you out."

At the door, he said, "Bye, hon."

I said "Bye!" without looking back.

I woke up in my bed the next morning. I opened my blinds and let the moody, gray morning light in. I received a text from him.

Him: *Going back to never bringing up sex again. You should do the same. I can't supplement what you've needed emotionally. Enjoy your day.*

It was something I felt immediately unsettled by, but eventually came to terms with. Then I was struck with the panic of *now what?* Who or what will be the next available resource for serotonin? We spent the summer using each other for intimacy like it was amphetamine. Every time we were around each other, there was a part of our brains that lit up like a Christmas tree. Our minds were dependent on such stimulus. His attention was half of why I was happy. Regardless of these concerns, I chose not to reply with anything persuasive or emotive. I chose not to reply at all. I felt like the worst part about the defeat was that, since he was the one who initially ended the romance, I felt like he was the one now in power. If I didn't give him a response, there was nothing he could ignore or say back, and that illusion of control was the only way I could feel okay. I tried this strategy for three weeks, distracting myself with bottomless mimosas at brunch or replacing him with other men. Whenever I was on the brink of losing self-control, I'd come to his social media just to see photos of his baby blue vintage track bike followed by an annoying caption like, "Gonna take this baby out for a ride today :)" or a selfie of him by the poolside with a bronzed blonde. But doing so only made me feel worse. I would find myself in this psychotic K-hole of obsession and felt alarmed by my own behavior. Did I catch the sickness? Months went by. Then, finally:

Him: *I miss you.*

A jolt of adrenaline struck me, a feeling that was once familiar. Was this an opportunity to offer a proposal to meet again? I had to choose my words wisely, lest they were my last. Then, reluctantly, I was ready to come to an understanding with the inevitable truth: this tug of war we were playing with each other felt purposeless and redundant. I wanted to reach into my chest and give away whatever it was that made me feel crazy for so long. I didn't want it anymore.

Me: i miss u too but u do not belong to me. although it was fun to indulge in that fantasy for a little awhile. maybe we should have never crossed the line. i guess this means goodbye for now xoxo

Unrequited love is worse than losing something mutual and real. With unrequited love, you don't get the comfort of knowing that you ran it to the ground. You don't get the privilege of knowing why it couldn't work. It's easier to move on from that. It's easy to make peace with knowing that you both tried your best. With unrequited love, you aren't granted the permission to explore. All you have is the heartbreak of having only the haunting possibilities and what could have been. As children, my best friend and I would go down into the muddy creek in my backyard and catch salamanders during the darker stage of twilight. It took focus and patience to lure these slimy amphibians into our cusp, only for it to slip through the cracks of our fingers and dive back into the shady depths of the bank, their tails flicking. Either we stayed to catch more, or we'd surrender to the idea that these creatures just didn't belong in our captivity. I had to let him go. What would have happened if I hadn't come over and slept with him? What could have happened if we withheld that decision for a little bit longer? It's the lingering, the haunting, that is frightening.

It was not love, I don't think. Love is ugly, but lust is, in a sense, more satisfying. Love is when the magic dies. Our affair was ecstasy hovering above the ugliness of love. What we had was something people in love do not. For a moment, we didn't care about where fate would bring us to. We were only happy in that moment. No matter what heartache or harmony he and I will experience in the future, we will always remember the summer when we shared mutual happiness for a short moment in time. And, even for those short moments, we were the lucky ones.

THE THIN BLUE LINES

I feel like my body has been against me my entire life. It never really blossomed the way it did for Mariah Carey in the case insert photos of her Rainbow album (1999). I was seven years old when I first examined her golden breasts and oily buxom legs. I was probably already too hyperaware of my body at this tender age but, still, even looking at my two sisters triggered an intense eagerness to become a woman. I'd often sit in the room with them as they got ready to go out for the night. With R&B playing on an old Sony stereo system, Winny would do her makeup with the help of a full-length mirror on the floor, with her extensive collection of M.A.C products sprawled around her. She daubed taupe-colored eye shadow on her eyelids and the towel that was once wrapped around her body would collapse and exposed a full C-cup pair of breasts. I couldn't wait to feel feminine. I couldn't wait to grow up.

One way to never feel enough as a young woman is to learn that puberty will eventually give you the breasts of your dreams but will forget about your reproductive organs. I was probably the only girl in the 5th grade to not have a period yet. I'd eventually get them, later in life, but they would be irregular and sometimes completely absent. I'd notice how other women had regular periods that seemed simple and easy; they all seemed to know the exact time their periods would come and which days would be the heaviest. It was the quintessential, cliché look of femininity: *Midol. Ben & Jerry's Cherry Garcia. Snickers Bar. Heating pads.* Being excluded from these problems should make me feel lucky, as many women would often say to me, but I would give anything up just to experience period cramps if it meant I'd feel normal. I would feel indifferent about my irregular periods and quickly acknowledged that I had no power over my own body. It came whenever it wanted, so I stopped keeping track of my cycle. One day, my period came in the middle of class. I was in community college and the hot spurt of blood oozed out when I shifted my body the wrong way. I thought that blood seeping through my light wash denim jeans was a perfect justification to be excused from class, so I wrapped a long-sleeved flannel around my waist and informed my female professor. She just told me to stuff my panties with paper towels until her lecture was over. I didn't go back to class. I didn't go back to college.

My twenties have been full of gynecologist visits that would leave me feeling more confused than how I would when I showed up to them. Blood tests, cotton swabs in my cervix, and annual pap smears would offer no answers. Eventually, I stopped making the appointments. I figured that if I had no control over how my body wants to work (or not work), I was going to rebel against it and do whatever I wanted with it. I had unprotected sex with a guy who I'd been seeing over the summer. Two months passed until I noticed I hadn't gotten my period. Initially, I thought nothing of it, as it was normal to me, but I was overcome by a gripping feeling that urged me to take a pregnancy test. I raided the cabinet underneath the sink to find a cheap drugstore pregnancy test sitting in the darkness next to a curling iron. When it showed up positive, my mind was so dizzy that I had difficulty swallowing. I paced the entire bathroom and walked circles in the living room until my roommate noticed. "You okay?" he asked, grabbing a cold Mountain Dew from the fridge.

"I'm pregnant."

"No fucking way, no fucking way. Show me."

We walked to the bathroom and I pointed at the test as he loomed over it. A quiet second passed before amazement turned into sympathy. He put his hand on my shoulder and said, "Well, congratulations."

I sent a cryptic text to my boyfriend, a quick "call me, urgent." that, in return, inspired him to call within a few seconds.

"What's going on?" he asked, panicked.

"How's work?"

"It's fine, Jen. What's going on?"

"I took a pregnancy test."

"Uh huh?"

"It's positive."

"So, what do you want to do?"

What do you want to do? It was a strange question to hear out loud. I had trouble processing the facts, the options, and—most importantly—the consequences; how every decision would affect us individually and as an entity. "I haven't really thought about it. It's... it's all just really overwhe—"

"Jen, I'm here to support any decision you think we should make, but we aren't fit to be parents yet."

The truth was difficult to digest, emotionally and mentally, but he was right. It was the kind of truth that felt as if I was a child with a toy that didn't belong to me. I was cornered until I had to surrender it. I laid my head on his chest later that night, both of us pretending to be asleep, but we could hear our hearts beating fast. We were wide awake.

As it should be for any woman, how I wanted to handle the situation was completely up to me. He was supportive and present throughout the decision-making, but I began to feel like it was out of moral obligation. I knew that becoming a father at this point in his life wasn't exactly what he desired. I knew that having this child would mean he would have to first learn to accept this new role. I knew he'd be a great father, sure, but I loved what we had, and was so afraid that having children so early in the relationship would spoil something good. And I was in no position to pass up on something good. I wanted our love to grow organically. Above all, I wanted to have him to myself first, at least for a while, before I had to share. When I came to the understanding that not having this child was for the best, my best friend gave me the information to an abortion clinic that she'd been to once before. I called to set an appointment for the soonest available date, which was in two weeks. The final days leading up to the appointment felt surreal. Living every day with a growing embryo in my womb that I planned to terminate felt weird. Smiling and having normal conversations with people felt wrong. I felt like I was lying. I felt like I was keeping a dark secret. Naturally, thoughts of regret became intrusive. I even began to feel maternal, like, even though this *thing* inside of me was unwanted, I still felt an instinctual responsibility to protect it. It was a part of me for a month and I protected it from the world, only to betray it, take it out of me, and give it away like a disposable mistake. I felt so anxious. At times, I thought that I was floating.

* * *

My mom always preferred the look of white walls. She believed that they could make any house look clean and modern, like the way living rooms looked like in interior design magazines—specifically the kind of interior design magazines offered to patients in abortion clinic waiting rooms. But, in reality, the white walls there felt cold and sinister. In the clinic, there was nowhere to escape the noise or to relieve myself from sensory overload. If it wasn't intrusive thoughts of doom and shame, it was the sound of phones ringing and pens tapping. It was CNN playing softly in the background with closed captioning. My boyfriend shook his leg out of nervousness, the sole of his Vans tapped on the shiny, tiled floor. He drew all over his hands with the pen from the check-in counter, jittery and scared. When a petite woman in scrubs called my name, I stood up with my legs feeling like gelatin. He stayed behind, continued to fidget with his hands, while I signed paperwork until I was put in another room where I was fed big white pills. There were women of all ages, ethnic backgrounds and class, but we all shared the same look of fear in our eyes. I was taken to a room where a technician did an ultrasound. *It* looked like a garbanzo bean. She asked if I wanted to keep a photo. I initially wanted to say yes, although the more logical side of me knew that this would only exacerbate the grieving process. I declined her offer. The trauma was a souvenir within itself. In the last room I waited in before the final procedure, I was left alone with a heating pad on my stomach. I was waiting for the white pill to initiate the cramps. The hallway caved in and people's faces turned into plastic. In a state of delirium, all the unprocessed emotions I tried repressing for the past month came out through a painful lament. A nurse that happened to walk nearby stopped and held me in her arms. "It's okay," she assured me. "It's alright."

Then the time came for me to sit in the stirrups, and the bright light made it hard to see the distinguishing features of the doctor. All I could recall was that he had white hair and thick bifocals. He asked me what I was going to do after this, to which I replied, "I'm going to get pancakes." That was all I remember.

There was nothing but lawsuit accident commercials and silence on the car ride home. My boyfriend, relieved now, tucked me in bed and left lunch on the nightstand. I slept for seven hours. I never felt anything after that day. Our relationship became stronger throughout the years. The topic of children didn't scare us anymore and being parents was a mutual desire. I stopped taking birth control and had unprotected sex with him for the next five years. Nothing ever happened. I visited the same gynecologist again. She told me that she believed my fallopian tubes might be blocked and so I paid out of pocket for an HSG test; an X-ray test to examine my uterus. They injected a harmless black ink into my vagina and then, on the monitor, we saw that the black contrast liquid only came out of one fallopian tube, but not the other. My doctor told me, "It's too early to be worried. There are plenty of options we can try before doing something as invasive as IVF. For now, let's try Clomid." *Clomid, an estrogen modulator. Used to treat infertility,* I'd learn through intensive research on Google. I dove into more WebMD pages. *Used by doctors to stimulate ovulation, a woman may be able to produce several eggs per cycle, giving more chances for pregnancy.* I used to have (somewhat) spontaneous sex. When we first started hooking up, I'd slather my body with body butter from Victoria's Secret before coming over. I once wore a garter-belt underneath my clothes the night before he had to leave for a business trip. He couldn't keep his hands off me. Now, while the passion was still there, sex became technical: *We have to have sex tonight. The chart says that I am ovulating and there's only a small window to get pregnant... Pick up dinner on your way home, xo.*

I tried two rounds of Clomid.

Still, nothing.

Something I stopped looking forward to was taking pregnancy tests. Somehow, my experience had never been a good one. Either I was a 21-year old alcoholic dealing with an unplanned pregnancy, or I was older and ready, waiting for the thin blue lines to appear. I'd daydream about the day the double lines would turn blue for me. I imagined it in the same way every chick flick had portrayed it: a wife takes a positive pregnancy test and waves the urine-drenched stick in her husband's face as they both rejoice in excitement. They hug each other and begin discussing which color to paint the nursery room. For me personally, I wanted something gender-neutral, like yellow. I hated idea that girls should be constricted to pastel pink and boys had to be specifically designated to robin's egg blue. It was such a sexist rhetoric. I also imagined holding my boyfriend's hand during our first ultrasound and seeing the irrefutable joy in his face. I felt like I loved him so much that I literally wanted more of him. I wanted to take his DNA and create a carbon copy of this man so I could have him forever. Sometimes we would lie in bed and go through names of our hypothetical child. "Joaquin" sounded rustic and menacing, or maybe something Latin and romantic like "Valentina".

"Penelope," I said.

"I like that." He nodded.

But, given my circumstance, this was borderline masochistic to do to ourselves. During these pregnancy tests, one blue line appeared and patiently I would wait for the next to fade in. I'd stick the absorbent tip in the heavy stream of urine and set it next to the sink. The instructions said it would take two to three minutes for the final results to appear. One line would come into sight, but never the other. I'd wait for five minutes and tried my hardest to repress the heavy blows of disappointment. Flushed the toilet. Disposed the test. I would either cry with my throat closed completely or be so overwhelmed with disappointment that I would counteract with apathy and numbness: *Whatever. What's new?* Each month brought a different wave of excitement and frustration.

Some months, I wouldn't even have the emotional capacity to do a test. I visited online forums to join a community of women who were also trying to conceive. There were women in their late forties to early fifties who were still holding onto the idea of motherhood. Some women had endometriosis and almost no chance of getting pregnant, but still had hopes of having babies one day. Others shared success stories: *Doctor prescribed me Clomid and we got pregnant on the first try! Sending you ladies baby dust on your journey! Never lose hope.* I had to leave these support groups. Reading other women's issues with their own bodies made me feel worse about mine. As much as I tried to recognize how unhealthy and mean it is, it just seemed unfair that other women I knew had gotten pregnant accidentally before. The right thing to do was to be congratulatory and happy for these women in my life, but there was a quiet sadness between jealousy and helplessness. The worst thoughts came to me during unpredictable times of the day. I felt like, if there was a God, it gave me one chance at motherhood like a sacred gift. Pregnancy was a sweater from Macy's and I gave it back to God and said "I don't look good in green. Sorry." I felt like maybe infertility was God's punishment for my decision to abort a pregnancy and if I ever wanted to try again, I would have to wait for it. Sometimes, as an attempt to keep my sanity, I would tell myself that there was probably an underlying lesson that I wasn't being receptive to. What if having children isn't what I wanted after all? What if God wanted me to adopt and care for a child that needed a home? I went to female friends for answers. "I think instead of worrying about how you can or can't have children, you should maybe think about why you want one in the first place." my friend Victoria once said, in a way that was not judgmental but helpful—yet still acerbic in delivery. I knew that I truly found someone that I trusted and loved. My yearning for motherhood came from a pure place and was not a heinous way to force commitment onto a man. I wasn't *that* kind of woman—the pathetic, desperate type. He and I *wanted* to be parents. The notion that there are kids in need of a home was sensible but still weird, only because it was said by people who could naturally have or—already had—kids. "Well, there are millions of kids that need a home." They'd suggest."Well, if that's true, why didn't *you* adopt?" I'd challenge them. Quiet pause. Blank stare. "Oh, right, because you never needed to resort to that because you have a working reproductive system."

Or even worse, women would try to console me by saying baffling things: *Just relax and it will happen. Have you tried vaginal steam baths?* I appreciated the words of encouragement but there was no nice way of saying, "I don't think sticking lavender up my pussy will help my very real medical condition" so I'd just smile and thank them. Herbal remedies sounded like a weird way to capitalize on such an awful condition. I didn't like to be told to relax. It was hard to relax. The clock was ticking. Every birthday felt like doom; it was another year I'd come closer to having the maternal door close on me for good. It was hard to *relax* when you were just a man's barren wife. He was patient and painfully optimistic. I got angry when he'd tell me to *relax* but I knew it could have been a defense mechanism to avoid the possible truth.

With the time I had waiting around to get pregnant, the idea of being a mother forced me to come to terms with my own relationship with my mother. Just like every Asian kid, my "tiger mom" never showed physical affection. This inadvertently caused me to grow up with intimacy issues. I held my breath whenever someone hugged me. Holding hands with someone was cute for a while until the sweat and heat from my palms made me wince and I'd slide my hand out of that embrace and walk alone. Now, I've learned that my mom wasn't actually as callous as I once believed. She just led with practicality instead of emotions. As an adult, this belief system helped me solve problems logically and I was able to separate reality from emotions. This is an excellent characteristic of transactional leaders. I liked the fact that I could address a problem logically and practically. But I'll also admit that it would have been nice to have been shown a little more empathy as a child. I was grateful for the lessons in pragmatism, but I'd sometimes fear that when the time comes—*if* the time comes—to be a parent, I wouldn't know how to give a fucking hug. And even if tough love helped me become a strong woman, it could have also raised a psychopath. Was I willing to roll the dice? What if I raise the next Jeffrey Dahmer? The only bonding experience with my mom that I remember was when she was cutting a mango in her palms with a kitchen knife and fed me the slices off the end of the knife's tip. She would then tell me: "Men are all the same and you should always be the one who emotionally gives less." It was barely advice. It was a power move. And let's be honest here, mommy issues are so much worse than daddy issues. With daddy issues, you could just compensate for that emotional hole with sex and you'd be fulfilled for the time being. With mommy issues, the consequences are far worse and less fixable: you struggle with being warm and maternal. If a bus hit me and I was on the ground bleeding to death, my mind would naturally assume that my mom would just panic at the circumstance and tell me that it was only a matter of time until my clumsiness would kill me. At times, I thought to myself, what if I become her?

What kind of mother would I be? I would either be the antithesis of her, or I'd adapt her best and worst qualities and instill them into my own offspring. Motherhood could change me as a woman and I wasn't sure if it would be for the better.

For him and me, we often wondered what would have happened if we kept our child. Would having been forced to care for a child neither of us wanted make us hate each other? We made mental notes of places we wanted to visit. I wanted to see Paris. He wanted to watch the Aurora Borealis in Alaska. I wanted to spend my life chasing dreams in the creative field. He wanted to spend his money freely on car parts and I was saving up for lip injections. Being young meant that we had every right to be selfish with our time and money. We didn't have to do anything we didn't want to do. Having children sounded like a wholesome experience to look forward to, but was I ready to sacrifice my freedom for it? I hadn't seen the world or taken it over yet. How could I focus on world domination with a teething child? Maybe parenthood sounded appealing in the hypothetical sense but not in reality. Whenever I'd take a negative pregnancy test and feel uncontrolled disdain, I'd implore myself to ask the big questions first. Motherhood was something that I wanted, but I had to remember that I had plenty of things to offer the world besides what my reproductive system could—or couldn't—do. I find that a woman can be fulfilled in other ways. I loved a man because it was his existence and adoration that I wanted forever. And, for the time being, I was already fulfilled.

girl
almighty